THE WINNING EDGE

"*The Winning Edge* inspired me in my unrelenting quest to continually strive towards excellence in the race of life. I believe that every man has a common vocation to be the best he can be as he journeys through life. This book spotlights athletes who are winners in the sporting arena and in life. Their stories reveal their precious struggles and the price that each of them have paid to gain a winning edge in the most significant game of all - the game of life. You will be encouraged and your life richly blessed in reading this book."

- Joe DeLoach
Olympic Gold Medallist, 200m Dash

"Sports people are the heroes of our generation. Peter Furst's book *The Winning Edge* gives us insight into the lives of sportspeople who have competed successfully at the highest level and who have found a dimension to life which goes beyond the final whistle."

- Stuart Weir
Christians in Sport UK

"*The Winning Edge* has brought together the collective experiences of top athletes who are dedicated to serving Jesus and who have something to say about the role Jesus has played in their personal and professional lives. Having been greatly influenced and encouraged by a great Christian player in my own sport, I recommend this book as a must-read for everyone, Christians and non-Christians alike."

- Jimmy Adams
Former West Indies Cricket Captain

"Our world needs heroes and this book is full of them. *The Winning Edge* is perfect for any person, young or old, who enjoys sports. It's always encouraging to read how God is pleased to work in these athletes because he wants to do the same in all of us. I'm always looking for the perfect book to encourage and inspire others in their walk with God. *The Winning Edge* is the book I give."

- Josh Davis

Triple Olympic Gold Medallist, Swimming

"The world is fascinated and inspired by winners. Peter Furst has gathered together some of the world's elite sportsmen and women and presented interesting insights in this captivating book.

"He has profiled men and women who have attained the highest sporting status in different parts of the globe. All are people who achieved success through discipline, determination and daring and all of them have that extra spiritual dimension.

"The athletes featured in his book have all experienced wonderful triumphs and the personal glory and acclaim that goes with sporting achievements. Yet each of these sports men and women featured have turned somewhere else to find the way to victory in their lives. Each of them has discovered the divine purpose for their lives. And each of them has found a personal relationship with Jesus that has turned their lives around.

"Peter Furst has provided us with a great service in profiling these great men and women and helping us find out what makes them tick. I found each story to be fascinating reading which will inspire readers to train harder, run faster, jump higher and aspire to become winners in life and throughout eternity."

- Dr Nico Bougas
Editor, Today Magazine South Africa

"Peter Furst eloquently describes the lives and loves of sportspeople whose prowess as athletes gives them a platform. These men and women - so admired by the sports fans - are just flesh and blood like the rest of us. The great thing about this book is that it points away from the gifts to the Giver."

- Andrew Wingfield-Digby
Chairman, Christians in Sport UK

"*The Winning Edge* is a great book of elite Christian athletes and people of sport sharing about their life, sport and faith in Jesus Christ. We salute these sportpeople for their willingness to share their life story.

"We all need to be stronger in our stands for Jesus and be willing to share in our sphere of influence what He has done to enhance our lives, and become a lighthouse of guiding others to a faith in Christ. We can learn a lot about how to do this by reading about the lives that have been changed in Peter's book. We see who gives the true 'Winning Edge' in life.

"This book will inspire you to be committed to go forth and share the good news of Jesus Christ and live a better quality of life each day."

- Dal Shealy
President, Fellowship of Christian Athletes

SPORTS STARS SHARE THEIR SPIRITUAL JOURNEYS

THE WINNING EDGE

PETER FURST

Lime Grove House Publishing, Ltd
Sydney, Auckland

Lime Grove House Publishing
PO Box 1704
Rozelle, NSW 2039
Australia

PO Box 37-955
Parnell, Auckland
New Zealand
Phone/Fax: 64 9 585 0023
Email: limegrovehouse@hotmail.com

First published in Australia in 2000
Second Edition 2002

Design and Typeset by D Whaanga-Schollum
Printed and bound in Australia by Griffin Press

There is a CIP entry of this publication recorded with the National Library of Australia

Cover photograph, Jonty Rhodes August 18, 1998 courtesy of Getty Images.

ISBN 1-8767-9872-6

To my dear friends around the world
who have been a great encouragement to me:
Jimmy, Josh, Joe, Ashley and Sarah

CONTENTS

INTRODUCTION

In contemporary society sports stars are revered, but each of them is actually just an ordinary person. In *The Winning Edge* some of these ordinary people share their extraordinary stories. In particular they reveal how their faith in Jesus Christ is central to all they are and all they have achieved. And this is not a faith just for sports stars, but for ordinary people – for all people.

What sets these ordinary people apart is the extraordinary circumstances in which they live, but the lessons we can learn from their stories are not limited to those who have become world champions or Olympic gold medallists. Because these sports stars are also ordinary people standing before God just as all other people, we can be encouraged and challenged by their spiritual journeys as they have learnt to rely on Jesus Christ through both success and failure.

As you share in the journeys of the sports stars featured in this book, I pray you will enjoy reading of the extraordinary moments in their careers – from unlikely victories to world record performances – but also that you would be affected on a deeper level as you consider your own relationship with Jesus Christ just as each of these sports stars have.

"This is how we know what love is: Jesus Christ laid down his life for us." (1 John 3:16)

Peter Furst
Sydney, April 2002

JIMMY ADAMS

USING HIS GIFTS

Jimmy Adams has tasted the sweetness of success aswell as bitter disappointments, both personally and as part of the West Indies cricket team. But despite whatever the fickle games of cricket and life throw at him, the Jamaican forgets what is behind and strains toward what is ahead.

In late 1994, Adams rose to the top of the world batting rankings after a remarkable tour of India. Playing in the three-Test series, Jimmy scored 520 runs at an average of 173.33, over 125 runs higher than his closest teammate. For the last two Tests Adams averaged 400, securing the Man-of-the-Series award.

During the final match, the twenty-six year-old passed the 1000 run mark with an unbeaten innings of 174. By the end of the Test, which was just his twelveth, Adams had tallied 1132 runs at an average of 87.07, behind only the late Sir Donald Bradman with the second highest batting average in the history of the game.

The Indians were shocked by Jimmy's ability with the willow and the leather, but those who had seen Adams' debut were not so surprised. Playing South Africa in April 1992, the lefthander made ninety runs and took four wickets.

Adams has many fond memories of the game. "There are so many that stand out for different reasons, like my Test debut, my first Test hundred, and winning a couple of Man of the Series awards. At another level, I've had wonderful times at both First-Class and club cricket.

"As a batsman, the hundreds you've scored always mean a great deal. It is considered the ultimate test getting there, and they really mean a lot to you as a player. More and more as I've gone on there have been times when I've been part of a team and the vibe has been fantastic. It's hard to describe. You're not necessarily winning, but you've been in a certain place at a certain time with a group of lads and you've just been happy. Everything has gelled and you've just been very happy. You come away wishing you could have kept that feeling forever. You've just enjoyed it, made good friends – it's been fantastic. Those moments rank as highly as the individual performances.

"Probably the most spectacular thing," he adds, "was my performance in India in 1994-95. Looking at performances by a few other teams in India since then has made me appreciate more how much of an achievement it was."

As a humble man, Adams reflects more his team than on any of his individual performances, but he certainly has had a few worth mentioning. Playing in Bridgetown, Barbados, in April 1996, he helped his team to a ten-wicket victory over New Zealand, taking five wickets for only seventeen runs with his left arm orthodox bowling. The following week he turned out with his bat in Antigua and added a career best 208 runs without losing his wicket.

Remembering the inning Jimmy adds, "Scoring a Test double hundred has definitely been one of the highlights of my career. Having also come at a time when I was under pressure to be in the team made it even more special."

Another special moment for the Jamaican came during the Australian tour of the Caribbean in early 1999, when he debuted as the West Indies captain in the 5th One-Day International, in the absence of Brian Lara. Adding to the significance of the appointment was that before the Australian series Adams had been out of the Test side for a year, and the One-Day side for nearly two - struggling with form slumps and injuries. The match, played in Guyana, is also remembered as one of unique controversy.

Chasing the West Indies innings total of 173, Australia required four off the last ball to win. Keith Arthurton bowled to Steve Waugh, who hit the ball to deep mid-wicket. As the Australians completed their second run the ball was fielded and thrown to the bowler's end. The crowd began running on to the field. Arthurton dislodged the bails, but Shane Warne was inside the crease. Waugh turned to complete a third run, hoping to secure a tie. To affect a run out and win the match for the West Indies, Arthurton only had to uproot one of the stumps while holding the ball, but before he had the opportunity the invading spectators had taken all the stumps. With the bowler unable to affect a run out, Australia successfully completed the run and tied the match - the result being declared by the match referee well after the close of play. For Adams, as captain, it was a memorable day.

On March 3, 2000 an even bigger honour was conferred upon Jimmy. After Brian Lara stood down as the West Indies captain, Adams was named his replacement. The appointment capped off a memorable month for the thirty-two year-old who had just captained Jamaica to a Busta Cup victory in the West Indies First-Class competition.

The veteran, who had already tallied thirty-nine Tests and one-hundred-and-four One-Dayers, was appointed not only for his experience, but also for his ability to earn the respect of his teammates. Then President of the West Indies Cricket Board, Jackie Hendriks said on Adams' promotion, "I am happy because I know he is a real fighter... someone who never gives up. I believe he will carry over the same sort of dedication and commitment he showed in the Busta Cup to the West Indies team, and that can only benefit West Indies cricket."

A delighted Adams said after the appointment, "Captaincy carries a lot of pressure, and I think it would be a little unwise to think it wouldn't add a little bit of pressure. Over the years pressure has not bothered me. I have come through some pretty tight situations in the past, and overcome quite a few pressure situations, so I am looking forward to the challenge.

"Being captain," he added, "was not something I thought about over the years; my ambition was to play well. It's one of the biggest honours anybody can have, and I am pretty honoured being asked to do it."

Adams became involved in cricket while growing up on his Caribbean island. "In rural Jamaica," he says, "kids spend half the year playing cricket and half playing football. I lived on a road where there were quite a few kids my age - and I had two brothers as well. Also as a child, I realised I could have dad's attention by playing cricket. He was into it and it was never a problem getting him to come and bowl to me."

As he grew, his skills developed. These saw him climb the ladder of representative cricket, playing under-nineteens for Jamaica and then the West Indies, and later being selected for the senior teams. Jimmy's First-Class debut came when he was just seventeen, against Barbados in 1985.

Being selected for the West Indies was an incredible experience for the twenty-four year-old from Port Maria. "It's hard to put it into words what it's like to play your first Test match," Adams says. "I didn't sleep for five nights. I just couldn't sleep; there was so much nervous energy. It had finally happened. But now it doesn't feel the same - you can't bring back that feeling. It's gone. It's a highlight in your career, but the feeling has gone.

"It highlights the fact that everything is a gift. I went through some hard times getting there. I had lost sight of the fact that what I was doing was a gift. You have a gift, the secret is to go and enjoy it. Do what you can, but leave the results to God. I drifted from that idea. I wanted it so badly, I'd forgotten that part of it. Since playing my first Test, it has highlighted the fact that everything, barring the spiritual, is only temporary. I don't get the same feeling when I walk out for a match now as I did when I walked out for my first Test match – I'll never feel that way again. I thoroughly enjoy playing cricket, but you don't get that great buzz that you had walking out for your first Test. All these good experiences - a lot of the things you are aiming for and that you might achieve – won't bring you lasting happiness."

Fortunately for Adams, he has realised that while so much is temporary, some aspects of life are eternal. "The relationship I have with Jesus Christ is everlasting. I have learnt about a peace of mind that surpasses understanding. I'm really looking forward to the day when I'll experience this peace of mind - this joy, this happiness, which the Bible tells us you can only imagine. Everything else we aspire to is temporary. I'm not saying you shouldn't aspire to them, but I think you should remember they are only temporary.

"As a cricketer, you'd be stupid if you got caught up in this life - and I've seen players do it. The life we live is a fantasy life; it's like *Alice in Wonderland*. You live in a hotel; everything is at your beck and call. You pick up your phone, you want food, someone carries food to your room. You want your clothes washed, people come and pick up your clothes and bring them back - and you don't pay for anything. That's fantasy land as far as I'm concerned, yet you've had players who have believed in it, got so caught up in it that when the day came that it was over, they've really struggled to come to terms with life as most people live it.

"Most of the things we aspire to are temporary. I aspire to a lot of great things on and off the cricket field, and I might actually achieve some of them, but while I'll be thankful for getting there, there will always be a little part of me saying, 'You've experienced some highs in your life before, and you know they're not going to last forever. It might last a second, it might last a night, two nights, a week, but it's only going to be a temporary thing. Enjoy it, but keep that perspective.' It helps keep your feet on the ground. It is something I find very important. Your spirit is the only thing that is going to be there forever."

Adams became a Christian in early high school. "I grew up in a Christian family," he says. "I was exposed to it from when I was a very young child. I made a personal decision to follow Christ when I was thirteen. The high school I went to had what was called an Inter-School Christian Fellowship group and I started attending meetings when I started going to high school. In my second year I decided to give my life to Christ."

Since that time his faith has developed. "As a thirteen-year-old, you're thinking more in terms of the everlasting life bit. You find that very appealing and deep down in your heart you know you are doing the right thing.

"More and more every day, however, I come to look on Christianity not just as something for the hereafter. I don't think you can have as good a life here now, regardless of the problems you see happening, without Christ. I see more and more of that every day and I'm thankful for it, because it actually adds to the whole experience. You're not just sitting down waiting for life here to end to pick up the good life in the hereafter, you're actually experiencing some of the joy of the kingdom here. In all the trials, the joy and the happiness, the tribulations, the sadness, whatever, you are still experiencing the kingdom here."

Jimmy's faith in Christ has moulded his philosophy on life. "I look on everything as a gift - something you didn't have to be given, but were given. I also look on my cricket results as gifts. I admit there are times when it is hard to accept some of these as gifts – I'm not going to say it's always easy - but you look on them as gifts anyway. You have successes and you enjoy them – they're given to us to enjoy - but you are thankful because they are not yours, they were given to you. You have disappointments and when you do it's all too easy to look around thinking there must be an excuse. I find it easier to cope by just saying, 'Thank you. You have all the results in your hands. You make all the decisions. You have a script written and I'm thankful whatever it is.'

"God knows what's good for you, it's just a case of being thankful. Looking at things from that angle makes it a lot easier for me, not only in cricket but in life as well."

The sportsman keeps his faith strong by reading the Bible and praying. "I don't like staying away from reading the Bible for too long," he says. "It has helped my Christian faith to have daily devotional time where I read the scriptures and actually have one-on-one dialogue with God.

"A lot of verses stand out," he adds, "but one in particular: 'In all things, God works for the good of those who love him.' As long as you keep Christ at the centre, it doesn't matter how bad things are. There have been times in my life when things looked grey and I didn't think things would work out, but they have - maybe not in the way I have wanted them to, but more often than not I've been able to stand back after a period of time and say, 'God, thanks very much. If I'd done it my way, I wouldn't be here now with what I have.'"

Jimmy realises cricket is just a game and wants to keep his focus on God. "God didn't just create us," he says. "He created a purpose for us as well. That purpose begins with Jesus Christ. Accepting Jesus as our saviour entitles us not only to eternal life with God, it also allows us to fulfill in this life the divine purpose for which God created us.

"The benefits of being a Christian," he adds, "far outweigh the benefits of not being a Christian. For me, what I do has been greatly enhanced by doing it with Christ. I say that unequivocally. All you have to do is take his talent and enjoy it. Take what he gives you, have fun, enjoy it, and let him do the rest."

Since the late nineties this resolve to trust God in all circumstances has been tested as the West Indies have under performed, and ultimately as he was dropped as captain in 2001 after the tour of Australia. "The last few years have definitely been a learning experience for me," Jimmy says. "I believe my character has been strengthened more by the years of struggle than years when everything seemed golden and rosy. I know from past experience that God will equip me to get through any situation he puts me in. My faith has grown, and my relationship with God has deepened as I have come to rely more and more on God. I firmly believe that without testing times this growth in my relationship with God would not have happened."

Despite the difficulty, Adams values the hard times because they have given him an appreciation of success that cricketers who have only experienced good days could not share.

The Jamaican also believes the right attitude is integral to working through both personal and team form slumps. During school, Jimmy enjoyed being given maths problems to solve. He didn't view the problems with despair when there wasn't an easy solution, instead seeing them as opportunities to develop. With this attitude Adams now approaches all obstacles, seeing them as positive and not negative.

"Generally I have always enjoyed challenges," he says, "and the last couple of years of my career have certainly provided them. It is very important that in the face of any challenge we keep our focus on God and representing him as best we can. He will take care of the results and outcomes. I try to totally enjoy the challenge in whatever form it presents itself."

While Jimmy has been enjoying the challenge, he has sometimes performed in the world's eyes, and sometimes not, but to him the results are ultimately irrelevant. "The nature of sport is very much a temporary thing. I can not afford to judge my worth based on what happens in a sporting arena."

Adam's worth is founded in his relationship with God, and the hard times have helped develop his patience, perseverance and faith. "I do not believe there is any situation I will face," he says, "that God will not use to mould me into what he requires."

MICHELLE AKERS

SURE FOOTING

Standing on the victory platform at the Centennial Olympic Games in 1996, Michelle Akers had tears in her eyes. The former American women's soccer captain explains: "I put my hand on my chest, found the American flag atop the stadium, struggled not to cry and belted out our national anthem. It was almost surreal. Extreme emotions - tears, laughter, disbelief, joy - all at once and all overwhelming."

Immediately following the gold medal presentation, Michelle was rushed from the platform to receive intravenous fluids for re-hydration. Even after this she was too sick to celebrate with her teammates. Some doctors advised retirement because of the Chronic Fatigue and Immune Dysfunction Syndrome (CFIDS) that had plagued her since 1991.

Akers was destined for soccer success, garnering All-American honours for four years at Shorecrest High School, and again for all four years while at the University of Central Florida. In 1985 she was named *ESPN* Athlete of the Year, and played in the first ever US women's match, against Italy, on August 18.

The style of college play and fierce international competition brought Michelle a seemingly endless battle with injury. "Some seasons I knew the trainers better than my teammates," she says. The health she enjoyed while preparing for the historic World Cup in China would prove temporary.

The victory at the 1996 Olympics was an incredible experience, but the game to remember was played in China in 1991. Decked out in red, white and blue, the US women's team was in the final against Norway. Akers was to be a key factor.

Michelle headed in the opening goal after twenty minutes. Eight later the Norwegians scored in much the same way. At half-time, coach Tony DiCicco challenged Michelle to take control of the game. "I went out and played as hard as I could. I never doubted we were going to win," she says.

When a Norwegian defender miskicked the ball, Akers took control. The keeper was out from her goal and Michelle remembers taking enough time to get the shot off at a bad angle. Planting her left leg, she passed the ball into the open goal with her right foot. Fifteen minutes later the US were the Women's World Cup Champions. Michelle was awarded the top scorer's Golden Boot Award, with ten goals in six games.

Many Americans didn't even realise there was a Women's World Cup, let alone that the US had won it. To fix this, Michelle became the game's spokesperson. Under the extra responsibility Akers became run down, and after some tests was diagnosed with CFIDS.

Incapable of facing the fact determination and hard work were not making her healthy, and crushed by an impending divorce, Michelle took refuge at her family's cabin near Seattle in 1994. "I always go to Seattle to get my head together," she explains.

Despite a wide range of personal issues to be addressed, the area that received the most attention was her relationship with God. Michelle began to realise attending church on holidays was a far cry from having a relationship with God. With little energy left she prayed to God: "You can have this stuff. You can have this body. You can have my life. You can have me. I've made a mess of everything." All she had relied on in the past was useless in the face of her illness.

Akers first entered into a relationship with God back in high school, with the help of an English teacher. Now as she refocused her life some of the peace she felt in high school began to return. Even though she feared being seen as some sort of spiritual fanatic, she followed through with letting God control her life.

The following year, the US defended its title at the 1995 World Cup. Aker's family and friends travelled to Sweden to watch her play, but instead saw her knocked out in the first few minutes of the tournament. In the game against China, Akers went up to head the ball and collided with an opponent's head, twisting her knee as she landed unconscious.

Her dad thought it would be too much after the CFIDS, divorce and four years of wasted training thanks to another injury. For Michelle, it was an opportunity to rest her body and renew her spiritual life no matter what the circumstances, through tears of disappointment and the subsequent US third place finish.

Ignoring her illness for years only made it worse. While developing her spiritual side, she began to read about the disease. She learnt how it affected her not only physically, but also psychologically. She knew she would never conquer it physically, but through a change of diet began to have more energy. She learnt of a related blood pressure disorder called Neurally Mediated Hypotension, common to CFIDS sufferers, and was diagnosed as symptomatic to NMH.

Equipped with a different approach to life Akers went to the 1996 Olympics in search of gold. "I went to the Olympics thinking I've been through this stuff before. It's not going to be much different from the other world championships I have played in. That thought was blown away. It was so different.

"I didn't realise the magnitude or the depth of passion the public had for the Olympic Games. We missed that in the two World Cups because we were playing overseas, and the World Cup is solely soccer. At the Olympics there were an incredible number of people involved in the Games, and people's awareness for the Games was great.

"The World Cup wasn't promoted, so no one knew it was going on unless they were hardcore fans. But not with the Olympics. The emotion and awareness of the Olympics overwhelmed me."

The Americans made it through to the final against China after a sudden-death extra time victory over Norway. "The gold medal game was a complete haze," Akers says. "That was not a fun game for me. We played the Chinese team who are extremely fit, very talented and very skillful. They hold the ball a lot. When you play China you basically run and run and run. Twenty minutes into the game I was ready to come off. I didn't think I was going to make it. At half time I thought I was done for sure. I thought, 'I'll keep going until I drop,' and I never dropped."

On the day following the United States' two-one victory, Akers wrote in her journal: "My thoughts are scattered and disjointed, but the sentiment and unforgettable memories will forever be embedded in my heart. My mind keeps returning to the past few years when I thought I was so alone, so isolated in my struggles and pain. God is so good. Through it all, he was preparing me for this moment, this experience. He took it all away, but he gave me back so much more."

Soccer used to be the number one thing in Michelle's life, now it was her faith in Christ. "Soccer has become a platform for me to talk about my Christianity, what Christ means to me and what he can do for others," she says.

Michelle sees God working in her life. "I achieved a lot of awards and world titles. God allowed me to experience all these not only to provide me with a platform for him, but also to show me that being the best in the world in my chosen sport isn't all it is cracked up to be. Trophies are literally empty vessels and for me to pour my life into them and seek my personal worth from them is ultimately empty, superficial, even tragic. Even though I achieved almost everything I desired career-wise, it didn't prove satisfying.

"All my life I sought to be a great athlete, and in some respects achieved what I set out to do. I worked hard and for the most part life has been pretty easy for me. When I first got sick, I planned to beat it. After three years, I ran out of resources and admitted I was fragile and vulnerable. Now I face limitations daily and am forced to reckon with a body that can't keep going when I tell it to, a heart that gets tired of pushing past the sickness, and a mind that can't find the answers to the pain.

"Fortunately, God doesn't leave me like that. I have learnt that God is the one who restores and builds me up. I have learnt to rely on him for my daily sustenance, wisdom and strength. He is there to pull me up and to fill the hole he has blown wide open in my heart. It hurts most times, but it is worth it. I am striving to not be so hard headed, so someday he can just whisper to me and I will hear him and quickly slip back into his stride. I live in this place where I seem to be constantly getting pushed around and knocked down, yet the personal growth I experience makes all the discomfort and pain worthwhile."

Michelle's success on the field continued in 1998, winning the Goodwill Games gold medal and being named to the Federation Internationale de Football Association (FIFA) Order of Merit. On January 30, 1999 Akers entered the history books by becoming the fourth person to score 100 goals in international competition, hitting one into the back of the net in the fortieth minute against Portugal.

At the 1999 Women's World Cup, some things had changed and others stayed the same. Held in the United States, this time the whole country knew of its team and came out in support. In the final against rivals China, more than ninety thousand people watched the game continue through overtime into penalty kicks at the Rose Bowl in Pasadena. Among the crowd was President Clinton, who told the team after the game, "It was the most exciting sports event I have ever seen, I cannot thank you enough for the gift you have given the United States."

Like many times in her career Michelle cannot remember the ending of the game, taken off at full-time after sustaining concussion. If she watches a replay, Akers will see each team take their five kicks, with the US goalkeeper, Briana Scurry, stopping China's third attempt. After 120 minutes, the United States won the World Cup by five goals to four.

Despite her absence at the moment of triumph, Akers' contribution to the win is widely recognised. "The fans witnessed one of the greatest women athletes in history," head coach Tony DiCicco said at the postgame press conference. "She's a true champion who let it all out on the field. Michelle Akers inspires me, and I know she does the same for everyone else on the US team."

"Michelle was the anchor for our team today, as well as the whole tournament," assistant coach Lauren Gregg added, "She's the heartbeat of the team. She's why we are where we are today."

Just over a year later as the team approached the Sydney Olympics, Michelle's body got the better of her, forcing retirement. "After winning in 1996," she announced, "I promised myself to never again play in the condition I was in during those Olympic Games. Since then, retirement has been a big issue with me and the decision to continue on with the national team has always been a prayerful and careful one. This year was no exception, and after the 1999 World Cup I wrestled for months about whether to play or not, but eventually decided to go for it because I knew unless I was absolutely sure I had spent every possible ounce of myself trying to play, I would beat myself up with second guessing for the rest of my life. But after battling back from a messed up shoulder and making the Olympic team, I found myself at the end – mentally and physically. It has been a hard fought year, and the decision not to go to Sydney was just as agonising, but I have huge peace in knowing I fought to the very end and have nothing else to give."

The thirty-four year-old's retirement marked the end of a fifteen-year career, made complete by FIFA's naming of her as the Women's Player of the Century. Since playing in the first ever US women's national team in 1985, Akers scored 105 goals in 153 games, but her retirement was inevitable. "It is a rare thing for someone with her injuries and illnesses to battle as hard and long as she has to stay on the best women's soccer team in the world," said Dr Mark Adams, the USA's team physician for the 1996 Olympics and 1999 World Cup. "However, this combination of problems and setbacks makes it very difficult for Michelle to play to the level she expects of herself. She's a warrior in every sense of the word, but it became clear to the team medical staff and to Michelle that this was the time to step back."

"The shoulder injury has definitely been one of the toughest ever," Akers added. "Not only because of the physical pain, the surgery, and the rehabilitation, but because of the mental anguish that goes along with trying to come back in a short time frame to make the Olympic team and then having to deal with setback after setback and complication after complication, all the while knowing every day and every hour counts as to whether you will make it back in time or not.

"2000 seems to have been a non-stop climb of Mt Everest with eighty mile gale winds at my face. But even in saying that, to climb a mountain, one only needs to put one foot in front of the other and hopefully, if you do that long enough, you reach the summit. That's how it has been in years past for me, and that's how I fully expected it to be this year. I knew it would be tough and I knew I would want to quit at times, but I have always been able to find something from somewhere to pull me through.

"Unfortunately though, things did not relent, and instead of catching a much-needed break as in the past, this time things only got tougher. I finally said to myself, 'This is insane.' I was taking IVs like Gatorade and getting injections and taking medicine for pain. Icepacks and tape were a part of my wardrobe. I was battling just to get through the day, and finally I injured my shoulder. I just said, 'Enough is enough. I am no good to myself like this, and I am certainly no good to my team.'

"In looking back, the journey has been amazing and I have been blessed beyond belief and imagination over the past fifteen years on the US women's national team. There have been World Championships won and lost, gold medals, travelling all over the world, more friends than I could possibly count, a renewed and emboldened faith, and a ton of memories that will last a lifetime. And the cool thing is that this isn't the end. I am saying goodbye to one huge part of my life, but I know this was all just ground work for more of God's amazing stuff to be done in, through, and around me in the years to come. I have run the race. I have fought the good fight. And now I am on to new and different adventures and challenges."

This chapter was written with the help of Jennie Chandler

AARON BADDELEY

IN THE SWING

Aaron Baddeley's name is expected to be mentioned among golf's elite for years to come. Despite many hurdles on his path to the top, the young golfer is confident he can reach the level his early successes promised.

The American-born Australian first attracted the golfing world's attention during the Australian Open in November 1999. The eighteen-year-old hit a final-round three-under-par sixty-nine to clinch the title, with a seventy-two-hole total of fourteen-under. Baddeley went head-to-head with then world-number-three Colin Montgomerie in the final pairing but was undaunted as he became the first amateur to win the Open in thirty-nine years.

Aaron remembers the moment: "I felt pretty good all day. Coming down the back nine I started to get a little nervous. I saw I was on top of the leaderboard. After I had a bogey on fourteen, I knuckled down and made sure I made some pars. I hit a great drive down sixteen, then a good second onto the green, and nearly holed the putt. That gave me confidence. Then I hit great shots on the last couple of holes. It was unbelievable."

Memories of the last hole are still fresh in his mind. "I was on the tee with a two-shot lead. All I had to do was get on the fairway, so I hit a two iron down the right side. I hit it perfectly onto the fairway. I then had a nine-iron shot for 144 yards, aimed it about thirty feet left of the flag, and hit it right where I needed to. Walking up to the green I knew I'd won it.

"It was a great relief and satisfaction. I two-putted and won. All the hard work I'd done over the years paid off. It was awesome. To finish on top was a dream come true. I'd always believed in my own ability. I thought I could win. I played the best I could, and it was good enough."

Baddeley's victory earned him praise from many sources. Former world-number-one Greg Norman said, "He has it all. You can see it in his eyes. He has the ability Jack Nicklaus had at the same age. He hits the ball straight and prodigious distances, he's a great putter, and overall a wonderful golfer. Ability-wise, at eighteen, I've never seen better."

That year's Australasian Tour leader Michael Campbell added, "He is incredible – he plays every shot without fear." Golf great Jack Newton also stated, "It's hard to imagine an eighteen-year-old has the mental ability to play with the world-number-three and stitch him up."

The Australian Prime Minister, John Howard, recognised Aaron's achievement, writing to him: "Congratulations on your great win in the Australian Open. To triumph with such style against fierce competition was a fantastic effort. I wish you all the best with your golf in the future. As the youngest winner of the Australian Open, and the first amateur champion since Bruce Devlin in 1960, your career is already off to a flying start."

Baddeley's achievement also caught the eye of the Board of Governors of the Augusta National Golf Club, who invited him to compete in the 2000 US Masters. Only one special invitation was issued for the major, and Aaron's name was on it. It was the first time an Australian amateur had been asked to play, and the first time since 1976 an amateur had received a special invitation.

"I was phoned just before Christmas to tell me I was invited," Baddeley says. "I was extremely excited, I couldn't believe it. It was a great Christmas present."

In the lead up to the US Masters, Baddeley played nine holes with Tiger Woods and Sergio Garcia on the eve of the Bay Hill Invitational. Woods was impressed. "At nineteen-years-old, there's no way I ever hit it that good," the world-number-one said. "I was spraying it all over the lot and just trying to get up-and-down and score. I wasn't as good a ball striker as Aaron, no doubt about it. He hits the ball very well and I was also pleased to see how nice a kid he is."

Baddeley missed the cut in both the US Masters and US Open but still believes his time in the US was worthwhile. "I learnt about patience and lifestyle. Being away from your parents makes you grow up. You can't buy experience, and for a nineteen-year-old I've had a great experience."

Baddeley's manager, Paul Galli agrees the time was invaluable. "What he learnt in six months in the States as an amateur is something any young amateur would grab with two hands. Seven US Tour events, two major championships including the Masters paired with Tiger for two rounds, practice rounds with all the top players, travelling the world… we wouldn't change a thing."

On November 1, 2000, Baddeley took the much anticipated step of turning professional. Less than four weeks later he received his first winner's cheque. Defending his Australian Open title, the nineteen-year-old became only the second player in the tournament's 100-year history to win as both an amateur and a professional. Baddeley also joined the list of back-to-back winners that includes Jack Nicklaus, Greg Norman and Gary Player.

Aaron dominated the tournament to such an extent that even two double-bogeys in his last three holes couldn't rob him of the title. "I had a tough year, a learning year, and people out there were doubting me," he said. "But I trusted my own ability and came out to win the Stonehaven Cup."

Runner-up Robert Allenby predicted Baddeley's future. "Aaron might well be another Tiger Woods given the time and space to develop," he said. "He's an awesome golfer and we should just let him go. He has everything to be another Tiger Woods and he's an individual. Australia needs another Greg Norman to lead the way in world golf and Aaron proved he's not pressured."

Baddeley's successful season continued at the Greg Norman Holden International, the richest tournament on the

Australasian Tour that year, sinking a twenty-foot putt on the first play-off hole to defeat Sergio Garcia. The two young-guns started the day as joint-leaders on sixteen-under-par and produced one of the tightest finishes in recent years.

The lead seesawed on the back nine, Baddeley one shot clear until Garcia birdied thirteen and fourteen to move twenty-under-par. The Aussie joined the Spaniard on sixteen, both then picking up a shot on the next to remain level. Garcia had a ten-foot putt on eighteen for the win, but missed. Both players finishing with a tournament record twenty-one-under-par and progressing to a sudden-death play-off.

"It was nerve-wracking." Baddeley said. "It was tougher than the Australian Open. I guess on the back nine here you can make birdies but the penalties are also much more severe. Also, it was head-to-head with Sergio. He knows you can hit a bad shot, so you have to make sure you keep hitting good shots and holing your putts. I was able to do that.

"It was awesome to win Greg Norman's tournament. Greg has really taken me under his wing. He has been on the circuit for twenty-five years now and his experience is invaluable. It was very special to win his tournament."

"I don't think I can play much better than I did today," Garcia said, "and Aaron played great, just good enough to beat me. It was a great battle."

As well as collecting the $A360,000 prize, Baddeley received a two-year exemption on the European Tour because the event was co-sanctioned. The money took Aaron to the top of the Australasian PGA Tour's Order of Merit, a position he held to the end of the summer, finishing with earnings of $A662,125 from seven tournament starts. Baddeley was also an obvious selection for the Rookie of the Year trophy, having become the first person to win two tournaments in his first year on the tour.

Aaron's grandmothers introduced him to golf at twelve, at the Croydon Golf Club in Victoria. It didn't take long to realise he had a gift and that his future would be linked with it. "I went from a handicap of twenty-three to six in eleven months," he says. "I gave up cricket and worked hard at my game."

This decision to focus on golf proved to be the correct one. At fourteen, Baddeley won his club championship. That same year he received a letter from Jack Nicklaus saying it had come to his attention Baddeley was a promising young golfer, and he wished him well for the future.

Aaron has clear aims in golf: "Every time I play, I play to win. But I also go out there to have fun. My goal is to become better than Tiger Woods. If Tiger is the best player in the world, and I want to be the best player in the world, then I have to be better than Tiger. Tiger is the benchmark."

To play golf at an elite level takes commitment. "I practice all day, every day," he says, "and go to the gym – just working as hard as I can to improve." Despite the sacrifice, Aaron has no regrets about doing what he does. "I like my life the way it is, and I wouldn't want to change it."

That Aaron has been able to reach the levels he has is largely thanks to his parents, Ron and Jo-ann. After the 1999 Open, it was revealed they had taken out a loan to finance their son's early career. "It's very expensive," Ron Baddeley said. "We're just an average family with an average income. I don't see it as any different to taking out a loan for your children to go to university. This is Aaron's university, what he's doing now. His subjects are out on the circuit."

Baddeley is grateful for the support of his parents, and is sympathetic to the anxiety his career at times provides them. "I think it's harder to watch than it is to play," he says. "When you're watching you don't have any control, but when you're playing you've got control over it and feel comfortable."

Aaron put off turning professional for nearly a year after his first Australian Open win. "I wanted to gain more experience before turning professional," he says, "Besides, money can't make you happy. You don't take up the game to win money, you take it up because you love to play and win. People that play golf just to win money are in it for the wrong reason. You've got to be in it for the love of the game."

Baddeley has not only gained attention for his three tournament wins, but also for his acceptance speeches after them. At the 1999 Australian Open he began: "First of all I'd like to thank my Lord and saviour, Jesus Christ. He was with me all this week, and kept me patient. I knew he was there, and it was great to have him to help me through."

For Aaron, his relationship with Christ is integral to who he is. "I've been brought up in a Christian family," he says, "and I've always believed - that's the way I was brought up. I never thought it wasn't true. Because of this golf is not my number one priority, my faith is my number one priority."

Aaron also cherishes the fact that no matter how good or bad he plays, God is always there for him. On the course and in life, his relationship helps him to keep things in perspective.

"You can always rely on God. It doesn't always work out the way you think is best, but he's always got your best interests there, and there's always something good that's going to come out, even if it's bad." Romans 8:28 sums up his thoughts: "In all things God works for the good of those who love him, who have been called according to his purpose."

Aaron is clear about what he believes: "Jesus died and took our punishment, and with his death he washed us clean so we can have an intimate relationship with the Lord. My relationship with God is more satisfying than winning because it's eternal, the wins last for only a little while."

As Baddeley's professional career continues, his resolve to trust God in all circumstances will be tested by both his successes and failures - each posing its own danger. But Aaron is confident that God has a plan for his life and despite what his golfing fortunes bring, he will continue to stay focused on the great price Jesus paid for him and the ultimate success that brings.

IAN BISHOP

HOLY TERROR

In 1993, Ian Bishop's life came crashing to a halt. Despite owning the West Indies record for least Tests to take 100 wickets, his career now seemed over. At just twenty-five years-old, the pace bowler had broken down with a stress fracture in his back for the second time.

Ian was born in Port-of-Spain, Trinidad, in October 1967, and grew up on the Caribbean island. "My parents got divorced very early in my life," he says. "My dad had to work long hours to provide for the family - there were three of us at that time - so I grew up very unscrutinised. But when I look back at my character, I think I was always a very compassionate person, combined with a little bit of rebelliousness.

"I never intended to play cricket for the West Indies. I always looked at Test cricketers as immortals, people with a rare talent in life. I could never aspire to be that."

Despite doubting that he would ever make it to the top, Ian continued playing cricket. "I went through the stages of youth cricket and under-nineteen cricket and finally, in 1986, I got into the Trinidad and Tobago senior team. A good friend of mine decided I had some potential. He negotiated a contract for me to go to England. I had one season in club cricket, but like my first year in First-Class cricket, it was very inauspicious."

Even though he had not played as well as he wished, Ian Bishop returned home for another season with Trinidad and Tobago, and then upon heading back to England received an unexpected bonus. "I heard upon landing in England," he explains, "that I had been selected to play for the West Indies team on the current tour of England. It was a great shock to me; it was way beyond my wildest dreams. I had never hoped to play for the West Indies; I never thought I was good enough. I got to my club in England, where I was supposed to be playing, and I just sat there at about three o'clock in the afternoon, soaking in this news. Lying awake in bed later, I thought the night was taking a long time to end and, before I knew it, it was six o'clock. I was still lying there awake, such was the absolute joy I was feeling at that point."

This tour was a remarkable occasion for Bishop. "Here I was on my first tour, a Christian and all that, trying to keep my faith quiet because I didn't want to offend anybody. Gordon Greenidge was strolling around the dressing room, Desmond Haynes, and the mighty master Viv Richards with his strong personality. I thought for the first week or two I would keep quiet; I didn't want to step on anybody's toes.

"Then a reporter came into the room and said, 'I'd like to do an interview with Ian Bishop; he's a young fast bowler on tour.' He started asking me questions about my childhood, what I expected to do on tour and if I had any other interests. I told him, 'Yes, I'm a Christian and cricket comes second to my personal beliefs.' The next day in the newspaper, there was a big headline on the back page: 'The Holy Terror comes to Town.' For about a year or two after that, big Curtly and others, every time they saw me said, 'Holy T, Holy T, how you doing?'

"But in reading the article, my teammates began to realise there was something about me. And I can tell you the heckling certainly begun after that, but God has a way of vindicating you. After a while they started to respect me for what I am; for what I believe. When we came to Australia that same year, Clive Lloyd realised I was Christian and he asked me to say grace at one of the Christmas dinners we were having. Everything improved from there. I thank God for that, because God has a way of keeping you. If you let your life bear fruit, people will know you are a Christian and what you stand for."

Ian first heard about Christianity as a child, but the turning point in his beliefs came during high school. "I was always bigger than everybody else," he says, "and we had these young guys at school who used to go about calling themselves Christians. They used to have these meetings at lunchtime, sharing with each other the gospel of Christ and what the Bible meant to them. I thought to myself that this is very sissy, and I used to go around heckling these guys. But every time I would persecute them or call them names, they would retort by sharing what they believed with me. Everyday I did that at school, I would come home at night and repent and ask God to forgive me. Then the next day, I would go back to school and persecute these guys again - it was fun for me.

"I did this for a while and then one day realised being a Christian is not soft. I started thinking about eternal life, and life after death. What does life mean? Where will I go after I die? It scared me a bit. I started reading the Bible and realised there's hope there. This life is not all there is: there is life after death.

"I decided to give my life to God; I wanted him to come into my life and be Lord. The final push was the example of my cricket captain at school. When he became a Christian, that was all I needed - that was my final push. I committed myself fully to God."

In May 1988, during the tour of England, Bishop walked onto Headingley for his international debut. "The first One-Day International I played for the West Indies is something I'll never forget, especially being scared bowling my first over. The first ball that came to me went straight past because I was so frozen with fear, just standing taking in the occasion."

Things improved for the bowler. Playing against Pakistan on New Year's Day 1989, Ian took five wickets for twenty-seven runs off ten overs in a Man-of-the-Match performance, helping his team to a seven wicket win.

After nearly a year of limited overs cricket for the West Indies, the twenty-one year-old celebrated his call up for the first Test against India in Georgetown, Guyana. Regrettably the match was a rained out draw, the debutant bowling just nine overs and facing one delivery with the bat. There were no such disappointments a week later however, Bishop snaring six wickets for eighty-seven runs as the West Indies cruised to an eight wicket win.

The right arm fast bowler continued to improve as he grew in experience. In the drawn three-Test series against Pakistan in late 1990, Ian earned joint Man-of-the-Series honours with Wasim Akram for claiming sixteen wickets at an average of 18.87. In the final Test he took five for forty-one – his third five wicket haul in just eleven matches. But Bishop's fortunes were not to continue.

"I was earning a good living," he says. "I was enjoying myself, seeing different places. Then the thing I feared most came upon me in 1991. I started feeling a pain in my back. I had heard so much about Denis Lillee and people like that who had broken down with back injuries - how their careers had ended or almost ended. I thought, 'God, what is this?' I continued playing for a little while, but the pain got worse and worse, until it got to the point where I had an X-ray. The doctor said to me: 'Look, you've got a stress fracture. You have to stop playing cricket. I don't know if you'll ever come back - it all depends on you.'

"I was due to tour England shortly after that. I'd never played a Test match in England and this was my big opportunity. Australia and England are the two epitomes of Test cricket - they're the pinnacles and that's where to go to be recognised. The selectors said: 'Look, Bish, you can't go. You've got to take a rest for a year.' I thought I might never play cricket again. I started crying for the first few weeks because of the bitter disappointment. I had sacrificed so much, I'd worked so hard to play Test cricket and, within the space of two years, it seemed to be all taken away from me.

"Fortunately I received a lot of support from my wife, who was then my girlfriend. She encouraged me. She said something I'll never forget. She said, 'It's not over until God says it is over.' I've never forgotten that.

"I started praying, 'God, if your purpose for me is to play Test cricket and to be a witness for you, then there is nothing Satan can do to come and steal that from me.' I sat, looking at the word of God. One scripture that came to me was Isaiah 53:5, which says that Jesus carried all my sicknesses. He took all my sins on his body and by his stripes I am healed. I had to read that scripture over and over for months until it became a part of me - until I fully believed God had healed me.

"It was really tough. There were times I was bitterly disappointed. Watching the guys play in England, I thought to myself I'll just give up because this disappointment is too hard for me to take. After about nine months, I started playing cricket again. I went to England. I finished off my county contract. I was just happy to be playing cricket."

In late 1992, Ian worked his way back into the West Indies side to tour Australia. That summer down under he returned to his peak. The tourists won the Test series, two-one, including an amazing one-run victory in the Adelaide Test. Bishop was in fine form, taking his best figures in Test cricket with six for forty in Perth; the West Indies claiming the match and the series with an innings and twenty-five run victory.

Ian also claimed his best One-Day figures that tour, taking five wickets for twenty-five runs in a Man-of-the-Match performance against Pakistan at the 'Gabba – the West Indies' opponents collapsing to all-out for seventy-one, his side reaching its target in under twenty overs for the loss of just one wicket.

Bishop was back, and at his best.

Ian took another five wicket haul in his next Test match, against Pakistan, in his home town of Port-of-Spain in 1993. He now had eighty-two wickets in seventeen matches, at an average of 20.02. But again Bishop's fortunes were not to continue.

"I played two Test matches and then broke down with a back injury again, this time on the other side of my back. It's always harder the second time something happens to you. The first time you think you might be able to get over it, but when it happens twice it takes everything out of you. I thought God had healed me the first time - that he had a real purpose for my life and I was just getting back into it. I thought: 'This is it. I'm not going to play cricket again. I don't know of anybody who has come back from two injures. Denis Lillee one, yes. A couple of other people one - but two? Life is over.'"

Ian gave up on cricket and went to England with his wife, watching on TV as his team played and Brian Lara scored a world record innings of 375 runs. After about a year, his wife challenged him that if God wanted him to play cricket, then he would be able to make it back. To everyone's amazement he returned to the international arena in 1995.

In his first Test back, Bishop fulfilled his dream of playing against England in the home of cricket. In the first innings, the rejuvenated bowler claimed five for thirty-four to secure Man-of-the-Match honours as the West Indies took a nine wicket win. Again defying the odds, Bishop was back.

The twenty-seven year-old's form continued throughout the six match series, finishing with twenty-seven wickets at an average of 24.03. In the third Test at Edgbaston, Bishop added the honour of becoming the fastest West Indies bowler to claim 100 Test wickets - in terms of games played – clean bowling veteran Robin Smith in just his twenty-first Test. Ian finished the second innings with four for twenty-nine, England collapsing to all out for eighty-nine as the West Indies posted an innings and sixty-four run victory.

Bishop remains thankful to God for what he has done for him. "God brought me back from two career-threatening injuries," he says. "He gave me peace and a calm assurance. God has given me a purpose in life. He has given me a focus. He has given me something to look forward to, a direction. We all want to succeed - we all want to be cricketers, footballers, basketball players - but nothing beats the miracle of salvation. The Bible says, 'What good will it be for a man if he gains the whole world, yet forfeits his soul?' (Matt. 16:26) Even if I became the number one fast bowler, what would it profit me to gain the world for forty, fifty, sixty years? Eternity is much longer than that.

"God cares about us so much. We just can't hide from the fact we were all born into sin. When we came into this world, we were born sinners from the day we came from our mother's womb. But God made provisions for us. We were cut off from God because of that sin, but God loved us. He sent his Son, his only son, so we could be redeemed and have fellowship with God once again. The Bible says if anyone would call upon the name of Jesus and believe on him, he will be accepted back into the family of God." (Acts 2:21)

Bishop fought hard for his cricketing success, but always kept it in perspective. "Cricket is nice," he says. "It was my job and all that, but my first goal is to share with people what I have learnt from God and what God has done for me. I could only play cricket because of him - I'm ever thankful of that."

Ian Bishop's international career ended against England in March 1998; his last wicket, then English captain Michael Atherton caught behind. In forty-three Test matches, he claimed 161 wickets; tallying 118 wickets in his eighty-four One-Day International appearances.

"Had he not injured his back so seriously early in his career," former West Indies paceman Wes Hall says, "Bishop would probably have been one of the greatest fast bowlers of all time. He had hostile pace delivered with a classic side-on action. He also has an indomitable spirit, as he has proven by coming back twice from stress fractures of the spine."

Despite failing to reach the levels many believe he was capable of, Ian carries on strong is his faith knowing that God's purposes for him extend beyond cricket. He is not bitter at what he failed to achieve, but rather thankful for all that God allowed him to achieve.

MICHAEL CHANG

HOLDING SERVE

In 1987, a fifteen-year-old walked onto the Association of Tennis Professionals (ATP) tour. No one was quite sure what to make of Michael Chang, but his talent and potential were obvious. Little more than a year later, Chang won his first career title in San Francisco, earning a world ranking of thirty and being named 1988 ATP Newcomer of the Year.

On the courts of Roland Garros, during the 1989 French Open, Chang upset tennis greats Ivan Lendl and Stefan Edberg on the way to capturing his first Grand Slam title. These unlikely victories are well remembered, the young champion coming from behind to win both. The game against Lendl in particular is viewed as one of the great displays of courage. During the match Michael suffered severe cramps, at one stage forced to serve underhanded. The teen returned from two sets down to take the epic five-set battle in four hours and thirty-seven minutes.

Remembering his French Open win, Chang says: "It came much earlier than we'd ever dreamt. The last four matches in particular were just played on inspiration. I never expected it; I don't think the tennis world or anyone else expected it. But the Lord has his way of working things."

At seventeen, the raw American became the youngest man ever to win a Grand Slam title, and still holds this honour. Chang also ended the year ranked among the world's top five, the youngest player ever to do so.

Over a decade later, Chang's presence is still felt on the tour. The years have seen him win over thirty titles with earnings approaching US$20 million, attain an ATP world ranking of 2nd (September 9, 1996) and become recognised as one of the most determined players in tennis.

"The Lord has taught me many things," Michael explains. "The one that comes up most often is perseverance - the ability to get back up and try again when you fall and fail. When I first came on the tour people said, 'He's too small,' 'His serve isn't big enough' and 'He's too much of a defensive player – he's not going to last very long.' They were entitled to their opinions, but to me it fuelled the challenge to go out there and prove them wrong."

Chang's faith gives him the strength and motivation to keep battling it out on the courts time and time again, and as his words suggest, his faith is an integral part of his life. From the beginning of his career he unashamedly spoke of the importance of his faith in God, much to the amusement of some critics. "Give it a few years," they said. "Wait until you've lived a little and see how you feel then."

Michael continued to stand.

At the 1989 French Open, as he received the winner's trophy, Chang thanked everyone who contributed to his success. He concluded by thanking Jesus Christ, saying, "Without him, I'm nothing." Along with the cheers came boos. TV commentators, coaches and even other players criticised him for "dragging his religion into everything." They advised him to keep his beliefs to himself.

Chang was unfazed by the response and continued to speak about his faith at every opportunity. It is what he said he would do when his career began, and there was no reason to stop now. "I've received so much joy, so much love and so many blessings from the Lord," he explains. "When something good happens to you, you want to share it with people."

Over the years, Chang has accumulated an impressive record of dramatic victories and comebacks. He has also suffered tough losses, including three Grand Slam finals. "You aren't always going to have great times," he says. "There are tough times and discouraging times. You have to go out there and give your all, whether you win or lose. I learn more from my losses than from my wins. In many ways, it's kind of humbling. I think back to the things I could work on. I learnt from them and improve.

"Over the years, I've learnt that the Lord only asks you to go out and give your best for him," Chang continues. "There's a confidence that comes in knowing everything is in God's hands. He is always in control and has a purpose for everything.

"I used to think if I lost it wasn't glorifying to God, but I've realised that when you lose people are watching to see how you react. They can tell whether you are sincere about your beliefs and where you stand by how you handle it. You get off the court after losing a tough match and in the press conference they'll ask you a few questions to kind of irritate you a little. They want to see exactly where you stand and where your heart is. I pray that the Lord will shine through me, that he'll give me strength and peace, and that no matter what happens my actions and words will glorify him.

"It's really important for me to keep my eyes on the Lord and not get too caught up in winning and losing," Michael adds. "God has his plans and his timing. It's comforting to know he understands everything I go through, and that nothing happens apart from his will. I'm learning to praise him in every circumstance, because he knows what's best."

Michael counts himself fortunate to have become a Christian during his first year on the tour. "Before all the fame and money," he says, "the Lord was teaching me his way. The wonderful thing is that as I look back at my life, I can see that even when I wasn't a Christian, he was still there looking out for me."

For Michael, making Christ the centre of his life is the most important thing. "My first priority is to be a Christian. I feel I've been put in this position to touch people's lives in a positive way. I look at my role as a tennis player as more than hitting forehands and backhands. For me, it's important to do the work I've been called to do. I want to portray a Christ-like image."

Michael became a Christian at sixteen after reading a Bible his grandparents gave him, and wants others to know about the relationship they can have with Christ. "When people read the Bible, and read it genuinely, they see it expresses a lot of love, a lot of giving, a lot of peace. It's something people, especially young kids, need. There's a lot of turmoil, a lot of peer pressure and a lot of temptations that can lead a youngster astray. I see my purpose at the moment as playing some good tennis, working hard and touching people's lives."

At 175cm and under seventy kilograms, Chang appears to be at a disadvantage in a game where size usually equals power. He constantly faces the threat of being overpowered, but has earned his place among the world's best by working to turn his weaknesses into strengths.

"I like being the underdog," Chang says. "It gives me a great deal of confidence to play somebody bigger and stronger and still beat them. My strength comes from that, and I don't back down from a challenge."

Chang spends hours on the court and in the gym, but has found there is more to fitness than exercise. "You work hard on physical conditioning, but you also need to take time to rest. Both play an important role," he says. "Working hard every single day is too hard - it just drains me. I always try to take at least one day off, or if I've been on a long trip a few days off. For me, rest is just as important as hard work because it refreshes my body. Then I'm up and ready to go, feeling good instead of just dragging myself along."

Finding that balance in physical conditioning is a key ingredient to success for a professional athlete. For Michael, his spiritual conditioning is even more crucial. "I do a Bible study first thing in the morning and also at night," says Chang. "Throughout the day I'll pray whenever, because the Lord is always there. He teaches me a lot through circumstances in my life, whether it's through a tennis match or some other thing that's going on."

The Chang family also helps him keep his focus. Michael is often joined on the tour by his parents, Joe and Betty, his older brother and coach, Carl, and Carl's wife, Diana. "We sometimes have our own Bible studies together and sit down as a family to pray," Michael says.

Growing up in a strong Christian family has helped Michael approach tennis with the right perspective. His mother explains: "We believe in doing our best and letting God take care of the rest. With that mentality, Michael does not put that much pressure on himself. He prepares as best as he knows how and it's up to the Lord to guide him on that particular day."

"I've come to realise," Michael says, "I need to go out and play my best tennis. The winning and losing is out of my control and in higher hands. Everything happens for a reason. I realise I'm not going to win every match, but if I work my hardest on the practice court and play the best I can in a match, that's all people can ask of me. That's all I can ask of myself. The Lord only wants your best."

Chang maintained his world-number-two rating throughout most of 1997, dropping one spot by year-end. The following year, battling wrist and knee injuries, he won in Boston and Shanghai but his ranking dropped to twenty-ninth. It was the first time since 1988 Chang finished the year outside the top twenty.

In 1999 his decline continued, failing to win a tournament for the first time in twelve years his ranking dropped as low as seventy-sixth in October. Chang's near two-year drought of tournament wins finally came to an end in Los Angeles in July 2000, when Jan-Michael Gambill retired from the final due to injury.

Addressing the crowd after the victory, Chang had to fight off tears. "I certainly can't remember a time when I've been that emotional in public since the 1989 French Open," he said. "We've had emotional moments in private over the past two years. Generally speaking, in public I'm pretty good. But it has been emotional for me."

The past two years had been the hardest times in Chang's career. "When I'm used to being at a certain level and I'm not able to maintain that, I feel like there's something wrong, something I'm doing that's not quite right. I feel now like my perspective has changed. It's a little bit more relaxed. I realise I am very blessed to have done something I really enjoy for so many years. It's very easy to forget about the good things when you go through difficult times in life.

"The last couple of years have been a kind of learning period," he continued. "I've tried to learn from it and become a better player. I'm trying to take things match by match, and every match I get under my belt is going to help me more and more. I feel like things are getting better little by little.

"Whenever you try to work your way back, it's never one huge jump. It's going to take some time. I don't expect to get back to the top just like that. It's going to be a lot of little steps. It's going to be gradual and I've got to be patient and put the time in and the effort to succeed."

"There are two things that keep me going," Michael said after losing his seventh straight match at the beginning of the 2002 season. "One is faith and one is hope. If those two weren't as strong as they are, I would sit right here and call it a career. But those two things are still strong. They're stronger than the emotions I feel now...

"I'm not afraid of coming back. I would regret it if I didn't give myself every chance of continuing. I don't know what the future holds - I may not win another match - but it's important to walk away knowing I gave it my all."

Chang's struggles on the court have not diminished his faith. "Like anyone, after going through tough times and discouraging moments, it's only normal to feel down. I've always said true joy and happiness come from the Lord and, as a Christian, circumstances don't affect that. Circumstances will always change in a person's life - sometimes good and sometimes bad -- but the Lord's love never changes and that is where a Christian's joy and peace come from.

"I look at my tennis career as a testimony to the Lord, to show that with him all things are possible. Champions definitely show they can achieve success in incredible ways, but I believe true champions show they can recover and come back too."

Victory isn't always on Chang's side, but with his words after losing the final of the 1996 Australian Open, he showed he is on the ultimate winning side: "...last and most importantly, I would like to thank the Lord Jesus because without him I wouldn't have the talent to play. It's to him that I give the glory."

This chapter was written with the help of Christin Ditchfield

STEPHANIE COOK

THE FLYING SCOTSWOMAN

Stephanie Cook went to the Sydney Olympics as a doctor who had become good at her hobby. She went to enjoy the once-in-a-lifetime experience, and never guessed what effect it would have on her life.

Cook was just an average schoolgirl – hard-working and reasonably sporty. Her first love was horse riding, and she also enjoyed running. "I was never a good sprinter," she recalls, "but whenever we did long distance running I would be able to keep going for longer than anyone else and did quite well. But I was certainly no remarkable athlete."

After school Steph studied medicine, first at Cambridge and then Oxford. In Cambridge she met a number of veterinary students who competed in the modern pentathlon, and even though she declined their invitations to join them, a seed was sown.

During the years in Cambridge another seed was sown and flourished. "I grew up in a Christian family and went to church at Christmas and Easter but that was about it," she says. "I can remember from an early age having my New Testament by my bed and reading bits of it. It was as if I knew there was someone there, watching out for me and looking after me. When I was seventeen, I was walking to a good friend's house with her and she started questioning me about what I believed. It was the first time anyone had challenged me to think about spiritual things.

"It started me thinking and questioning what I believed and what my own faith was. My friend went to a youth group in Cambridge and I started going with her. There was never one defining moment when I thought, 'Yes, that's it. Everything has changed.' My faith has always been there although it hadn't been clarified in my own mind, but during that period everything started to make more sense."

Between school and university, Steph spent six months in Israel. It was an important time of consolidating her faith, and placed the biblical accounts of Jesus in their historical context.

Back in Cambridge as an undergraduate there was plenty of teaching, fellowship and encouragement at her church, the university Christian Union and college chapel services. These were not the only places Cook expressed her faith. "I wanted to be a Christian in other situations rather than being totally involved in Christian things. I was involved in sport and tried to be a Christian representative, to be a witness as much through my actions as my words."

When Steph commenced her clinical medical studies in Oxford, running was her main sport. Before she left university she was selected for England as a cross-country runner.

Shortly after arriving at Lincoln College, Oxford, she saw a poster inviting people to try modern pentathlon.

Modern pentathlon consists of shooting, fencing, swimming, horse riding and running – usually all held on one day. The sport was born from the bravery of a young French cavalry officer in Napoleon's ranks during the Franco-Prussian war in the nineteenth century, so the legend goes. The officer was sent on a horse he had never ridden before to deliver a message. En route he faced a fencing duel, shot the soldier who killed his horse and ran to continue his mission, finally swimming across a river to complete it. Pierre de Coubertin, the French founding father of the modern Olympics, was so moved by the tale he came up with the idea of the pentathlon, which was introduced at the 1912 Games.

Steph was on her way to international recognition as a runner. She had also done quite a bit of riding, but had not swum competitively since school and had never shot nor fenced. Despite this she attended a few training sessions and took part in a varsity match for novices - and won. However, at this stage her top priority was her studies - she was running seriously and no more than dabbling in pentathlon.

In 1997, her final year at university, Steph represented Oxford in four sports - athletics, cross-country, fencing and modern pentathlon. She gained her first England running vest for cross-country and was also selected to compete for Great Britain in modern pentathlon. There was also the matter of her medical finals to be fitted into the schedule.

She came fourth in her first international pentathlon competition, but it was a rather low-key event. The following week she competed in a World Cup event in Hungary, and when she came fifth people began to notice her.

When Cook started work as a junior doctor, she was an international pentathlete but had so far missed out on competing in a major championship, having been a non-travelling reserve for the British team for both the European and World Championships in 1997.

"Having got so close," she says, "I wanted to take it one step further. In retrospect, if I had been selected for the World Championships I might have thought that was enough and not gone any further. As it was, I felt I had not really fulfilled my potential."

The following year, while working long hours as a junior doctor, she continued training and competing. She was selected for the 1998 World Championships in Mexico, coming eighth individually as well as gaining team silver and relay bronze medals.

In 1999, Cook was the British modern tetrathlon champion (pentathlon without the riding). In the modern pentathlon European Championships she was tenth in the individual competition as well as taking a team silver. At the World Championships she won a team silver and a relay gold.

A chance meeting with a consultant surgeon led to the offer to do medical research, which was more flexible than a clinical post for her training and competing. A chance meeting it may have been, but for Steph it was "God opening a door. There were a few things that happened that led me to take pentathlon a bit further. This was a chance meeting but I believe God's hand was in it. I moved to Guildford, not really knowing what to expect and feeling quite apprehensive. I was wondering what I was doing there but it seemed to be what God was telling me to do."

Cook qualified for a Sports Council lottery grant that enabled her to train fulltime for the 2000 Olympics. In March 2000, she secured her Olympic qualification by winning gold at the Mexico World Cup, and completed her preparations by taking the individual silver medal (plus relay gold and team silver) at the European Championships in Hungary, and followed these with a ninth place and two team silvers at the World Championships.

Steph set out for the Olympics determined to make the most of the experience. "My preparation for Sydney had gone well," she says, "and my competitions had been consistently good. Just after we arrived in Sydney, the new world rankings came out and I was ranked joint number one in the world.

"Before that I thought, 'What do I really want to achieve in Sydney? What would be a good thing for me to achieve?' I remember thinking whatever happened in the Olympics it would be nice at some stage to be world-number-one. I had been in the top ten for some time but to be number one would be something quite special. I wasn't expecting it at that point.

It was quite strange and, to start with, it seemed to put increased pressure and expectation upon me.

"But I turned it around and started using it in a positive way. It meant I had performed consistently well during the year and there was no reason why it shouldn't be the same in Sydney."

As Cook left for Sydney, she took with her a book of Bible quotes a friend gave her, organised into a verse for each day of the training camp and the Games. "It was lovely for me to have them each day as a focus, and to build them into my quiet times. God was constantly there as a focus for the day. I find it very important to be disciplined in my Christian life and to have regular quiet times each day. It can be difficult when you are away and don't have the usual fellowship and encouragement from a church."

Steph's first memorable moment from the Olympics happened as they began. "We were very lucky to go to the opening ceremony. Many of the Great Britain team were still based on the Gold Coast, and team policy was for athletes not to travel to Sydney just for the opening ceremony. But the pentathlon team thought it would be beneficial for us to go down and get a feel for the atmosphere and experience the village before returning the following week for competition. I'm sure it was the right thing to do. It was an amazing experience to walk into the stadium as part of the British team."

With the fun over, then came business. There are no heats in the modern pentathlon. The twenty-four competitors simply compete until one of them is crowned champion. The 100m final lasts less than ten seconds - one mistake and you are gone. In contrast, the modern pentathlon Olympic final consists of twenty pistol shots, twenty-three sword fights, a 200m swim, a round of show jumping and a 3000m run. One mistake makes little difference - no one can be perfect at everything. Endurance is what is needed. Fortunately Steph developed endurance working long hours as a doctor.

Sunday October 1, at 6:45am the event got under way. Despite the time there was quite a crowd in the arena. The first event was shooting. Steph scored 178 target points, the leader had 185. "I was pleased with the shooting," she says. "It was within the range of what I expected to shoot. I had hoped for 180, so 178 wasn't too bad. That put me in eighth place and still in touch with the leaders."

After a one hour break, the fencing began. The change from shooting to fencing is difficult. Mentally the competitors want to be calm and controlled for the shooting and then aggressive for the fencing. Not being a naturally aggressive person, Steph has to work hard to psych herself. This is not her strong event, so holding her own was the aim.

Each person fences the other twenty-three competitors. Cook started with a win over teammate, Kate Allenby, but lost her next four fights. "When I found myself five hits into the competition and four down, that was the only time in the whole day I felt anxious. It was make-or-break time. I needed a mental turn-around. I needed to go into the sixth bout with the same confidence I started with." She finished the fencing with ten victories and slipped to fourteenth place overall.

"I was pleased how the fencing went," Steph says. "It was solid. I had been able to hold my own against the other competitors as far as points were concerned, but because I had dropped to fourteenth place I knew anyone who didn't know me or what I was capable of in the later events would write me off at that stage. That didn't worry me. I was just pleased I had my best events to look forward to."

By midday the competitors were at the Olympic pool for three heats of eight swimmers, graded according to past performances. Steph finished the first 200m heat in a personal best, 2:26. "I was hoping for 2:25, but you can't grumble about that." She still lay in fourteenth overall but had closed the gap.

"I knew as long as I had a decent ride I could be in with a chance. In pentathlon it's never worth thinking about where you might end up until the riding is over because that can shake things up completely."

For the show jumping, competitors were confronted with twelve Australian horses they had never seen before. Each horse goes around the course with two competitors. The event is harsh. Three competitors were eliminated and got no points, their medal hopes destroyed.

Steph drew a horse called Wagga Wagga. Her partner rode first, and while Steph watched she collected several penalties. "I was thinking, 'Now I have got to get on this horse and try to make it go better.' I thought I would do ok but my chances of a medal seemed to be slipping away. I thought the horse would probably knock too many poles down. I spent most of the twenty minutes preparation time trying to calm it down. I didn't have many muscles left in my arms after the ride as the horse was very strong. I was thrilled to come away with only two fences down." Cook moved to eighth.

Just before 5pm the final event, the 3000m, began. Points convert to time. The leader starts first, then everyone else so many seconds later according to the points they have accumulated in the previous four events. Steph started forty-nine seconds behind the leader.

"Over the summer, in other competitions, I had made up quite a lot of seconds on other people. I believed if I was within a minute of the leaders, I stood a chance of running into the medals. What you have no control over, though, is how fast the other people are going to run. The crucial person was Emily DeRiel, the leader. I knew she had been training at altitude before arriving in Australia, and I had not seen her run since the World Championships in June. All I could do was run my own race and hope it would be enough. The important thing was to pace the race right. If I could do that then, God willing, I would still be able to pass Emily at the end."

By the first corner Steph had passed the girl in seventh. After 500m she had cut the lead to thirty-three seconds. By halfway she was fourth. Then she passed Mary Beth Iagorashvili. "That was one of the most exciting moments," she remembers, "when I knew I had a medal. It was hurting quite a lot at that stage and it was quite tempting to leave it there and settle for a bronze medal, but I thought no one would forgive me if I didn't go for it."

With 500m to go Cook passed Kate Allenby to move into second, and with 300m left overtook Emily deRiel to take the lead, holding it to win by two seconds. At 5.30 pm, almost twelve hours after the competition started, the British national anthem was played as Steph Cook wore the gold medal.

Across the main road from the baseball stadium – where the afternoon events had taken place – the men's marathon was finishing. That was immediately followed by the closing ceremony. There was no way Steph was missing out on that final victory parade.

She had set out for Sydney as a doctor who was rather good at her hobby, but returned home as a celebrity. She was totally unprepared for the demands on her time. There were TV appearances, endless interviews, awards ceremonies, charity functions… There was the shock of being recognised in the supermarket, being stopped in the street.

Some of it has been fun, some of it exhausting. "I cope in the only way I know how – by being me. It was incredibly difficult after Sydney. Overnight it felt as though my life was totally turned upside down, and yet I was still the same person with the same principles and values as always."

Keeping her focus right has helped too. "When I took up modern pentathlon, it was obvious God had given me gifts for the sport. I just tried to use the ability God had given me to the full and hopefully bring some glory to his name in the process."

Cook continued her sporting career for less than twelve months after her golden success in Sydney, choosing to bow out at the 2001 World Championships and resume her medical profession. The championships, held in Somerset, provided a fairytale ending to her equally remarkable career.

Trailing leader, Italian Claudia Cerutti, by just eleven seconds at the beginning of the 3000m run, Steph comfortably seized the World Championship gold – crossing the line 500m ahead of her rival. The swansong was made complete by a golden hat-trick as Cook helped Great Britain also win the team championship and the team relay titles.

Cook's decision to leave her sporting life behind after so short a time at its pinacle was inspired by Eric Liddell, the Scottish sprinter whose story is told in *Chariots of Fire*. Liddell shot to fame at the 1924 Olympics when he refused to compete in the 100m because the race was held on a Sunday. Instead he entered and won gold in the 400m. But the rest of Liddell's story – and the part that most inspired Steph – is not as well known. After winning gold, the Scotsman retired from athletics and became a missionary in northern China. There he stayed until dying at forty-three in a Japanese prisoner of war camp.

"I feel I can relate to an awful lot of Eric Liddell," Cook says. "The gifts that I have been given do not stop at what I have done in the sporting field. There is a verse from the Bible that Eric Liddell referred to before his race at the Paris Olympics: 'They that honour me, I will honour.'

"I can completely understand that. Liddell had a great gift to be able to run in the way he did. He used his talent to the full in the Olympics. But that wasn't the be all and end all of life for him. He used the gifts that God had given him and then he did something else. I feel I have done that part of my life and now I'm ready to move on...

"I'm a relatively private person. I never went into the pentathlon to win medals or thinking I would become famous," Cook adds. "I'm glad my success has brought pleasure to other people. I'm glad it has acted as an inspiration to other people. But it isn't about getting in the papers, even though it is great when people write nice things about you. Now I want to use my profile to do something useful."

This chapter was written by Stuart Weir

ADRIAN DAVIES

MIXED FEELINGS

Welsh pride was at a peak in the 1970s, partly due to the country's rugby team. The pack was formidable, and behind the scrum every player was a potential match-winner. The team brought Wales an unprecedented period of success.

For schoolboys, every lunchtime was an opportunity to become their favourite player. In their dreams they were putting on the red Welsh jersey and stepping on to the hallowed turf at the Cardiff Arms Park.

For most the dream was just that, but for Adrian Davies it became reality. "I spent so many hours watching and playing games," he says. "Every kid growing up in the 70s, in the era of that successful Welsh team, wanted to be part of it. It gives me a great sense of satisfaction having achieved it."

From an early age it was obvious Adrian had talent. At eleven he captained his East Wales rugby side. During the Welsh Rugby Football Union Centenary, as captain of East Wales he got to run on to the pitch at the Arms Park with Jeff Squire, then captain of Wales. That moment fuelled his desire to play.

He was equally good at football and rugby, playing both most weekends. Before turning sixteen he had already represented his country in the two. He was invited for trials with Leeds United and Sheffield Wednesday, but decided to stay at school and not pursue professional football. In making this decision he also, unconsciously, decided to concentrate on rugby.

After finishing high school, Davies took a year off to work and play rugby for Neath, before going to University. "I was very fortunate the management of Neath thought if you were good enough, age did not matter. So at eighteen I was thrown into possibly the best side in Wales at the time.

"Neath was a hard and aggressive team. The game was based on physical intimidation of the opposition. It was great for me as a young whippersnapper to play number ten in that team. There were enough winners around to show me what was required. That certainly developed my mental attitude and my approach to rugby."

It was a wonderful opportunity for a rugby player, but not the easiest environment to stand up as a Christian. "It was a lot easier having my elder brother, Graham, in the dressing-room. We had the respect of the guys as rugby players and that is where the respect starts. As a result of that when the time arose and as friendships grew we were able to put across what we believed. We still got some stick though."

Adrian grew up in a Christian family, but that didn't make him a Christian. Rather, he sees his coming to a personal Christian faith as a process. "The seed was sown in my life out of respect for mum and dad and what their faith gave them. They were very strong Christians and it was always there in the family as a very strong influence. Most of the time I wasn't allowed to play rugby on Sundays. I didn't always agree with that.

"The development of my own faith came with the gradual breaking down of the barriers I put up. When I was seventeen, in human terms I had absolutely everything. I had passed my high school exams. I had played football and rugby for Wales. I had a pretty girl friend. Yet I knew there was something more.

"One Sunday, a girl I had known for a long time spoke at church. From the outside she had achieved nothing like I had. She stood up the front and said, 'I have decided to follow Jesus, and for him to be at the centre of my life from now on.' She looked so happy. I realised I didn't have that presence of Christ in my life. I knew I had to face the issue and shortly after that, I became a Christian. That is how I made the decision for myself, however I feel I had been drip-fed Christianity all my life up to that point."

As Adrian studied a degree in Geography and Land Economy at Cambridge University, rugby continued to influence most of his life. "Obviously things have changed since the game has gone professional, but at that stage of my career it was a massive opportunity for me to develop. I cannot speak highly enough of the Cambridge University Rugby Club. We trained just about every day. To play against top clubs while at the same time getting a degree was an amazing privilege. It was so much fun during my four years there that it probably took four years to get it of my system. I still go back every year to do some coaching."

The highlight of the season is the varsity match against Oxford. Adrian's record is two wins and two defeats, including a win as captain in his final year. That year he also went back to playing football and played in the football varsity match.

After university Adrian went back to Wales and moved from Neath to Cardiff, "mainly because of the friends I had at Cardiff," he says. "Cardiff is the biggest club in Wales, and it's always a challenge to play there."

Big club or not, Cardiff finished bottom of the ladder in Adrian's first season and would have been relegated but for a reorganisation of the league. Then Alec Evans was appointed coach, some new players came and gradually things turned around. During the four years he spent at Cardiff, the club won the Welsh Cup and also the Heineken League.

One of the highlights was reaching the final of the inaugural European Cup. Cardiff played Toulouse, who dominated the early part of the game with two tries. However four Davies penalties brought Cardiff back into the game. With Toulouse 15-12 up and the full eighty minutes gone, Cardiff got a penalty forty-three metres out. Adrian slotted it home to take the game into extra time. He kicked a sixth penalty, but Toulouse won 21-18 with a penalty in the last minute of play.

Adrian recalls an unusual event at Cardiff. "One training session I was with a group of guys doing a contact session, and I was getting a pasting every time. As I held the contact pad, the guys were running at me and I was being trampled on again and again. After this had gone on for nearly an hour, Andy Booth came in and quite fairly knocked me over. I reacted by throwing a massive haymaker. In all my years of rugby I never looked for a fight, but this time I completely lost it.

"The funny thing was that Boothie didn't swing back. Everyone just stopped and looked at me as if to say, 'What has Adrian done?' They could not believe I had lost it. Then they fell about laughing. Ironically the impact of that was positive. I apologised and so on, but it showed I was human and keen to compete and develop myself. If someone else had done it they wouldn't have batted an eyelid, but it was not what they expected of me. Boothie is still a friend of mine and even ten years later he still teases me about it."

In 1990, Adrian was selected to the bench for Wales against the Barbarians, a game given full international status. "In the second half Mark Ring came off and I replaced him. I nearly fell down the stairs rushing from my seat I was so excited. I was desperate to get on the field. It was absolutely fantastic, everything I had worked for. It had been a desire of mine all through my life and to achieve it was very special."

His next cap was not the most famous day in Welsh rugby. On tour in Australia in 1991, Wales lost 6-63. It was impossible to make much impression in a one-sided game in which the backs struggled for possession.

He made four appearances in 1993 – two on tour in Zimbabwe, which were won 42-13 and 35-14, a 55-5 win over Japan and an embarrassing defeat at home to Canada by 24-26. The following year he played in a 19-15 victory over Fiji but still wasn't selected for any of the Five Nations games.

The highlight of his career was playing in the 1995 World Cup in South Africa. Wales lost to New Zealand in a game that Adrian did not play. He was in the team when Wales beat Japan 57-10 with Neil Jenkins kicking twenty-two points. Adrian's role was to keep turning Welsh possession into scoring opportunities, and he did it well as Wales ran in seven tries.

Wales' final group stage match was against Ireland at Ellis Park with the winner progressing to a quarterfinal with France. Neither side played to its best, but Ireland squeezed through 24-23. Adrian got on the scoresheet with a drop goal.

The World Cup is still clear in his mind. "I have such contrasting memories of the 1995 World Cup, the most vivid one being the dressing room after the 23-24 defeat to Ireland. There was an overwhelming sense of disappointment and that we had not done ourselves justice. We all knew we should have won the match.

"I had been waiting to play in a game of that importance for the six years since being in the Welsh squad. I prayed before the game, in the shower, but then things didn't work out. Afterwards I did ask God why, and I don't really know the answer even now. It was also such a contrast to the thrill of getting into the Welsh team for the first match against Japan and being part of such a great performance.

"During the World Cup I went to church in Bloemfontein, which was really helpful. The service went so long the boys sent a search party looking for me. The time in Bloemfontein was actually the closest I've ever felt to God when on tour. My prayer and Bible study times were very special."

Following the 1995 World Cup, the authorities decided players in Rugby Union, an amateur game for over 100 years, could be paid as professionals. Richmond was quickly off the mark, offering Adrian a contract.

"The decision to go professional was not, at the time, as big as it might have seemed. It may surprise people to know the motivation was ambition, not money. I still passionately wanted to play for Wales and knew people like Neil Jenkins – my main rival for the number ten shirt - were effectively professional and so if I wanted to compete, I had to be a professional rugby player.

"I also wanted the challenge of seeing how good I could be if I had the chance of developing my ability to the full through full-time training. I knew I could perform at a higher level, given the time to practise. Financially, the offer was good and meant the decision to give up my profession was not as hard as it might have been.

"What was a massive decision was to leave Cardiff. We were a very successful team and I was really enjoying playing there. It was a huge wrench for me to leave. In the end I left Cardiff because it was a little slow in seeing the potential of professional rugby."

His three years at Richmond were a mixed bag. There was the excitement of the new professional era. There was the challenge of playing against the top players from England and beyond, every week. There were some brilliant performances. There were also three knee operations and ultimately losing the battle to recover the fitness required for top level rugby, as well as the liquidation of Richmond Rugby Club.

A particular disappointment of this period was not getting back into the Welsh team. The injuries did not help, and for part of the time Adrian suffered from a deliberate policy to give preference to players who were based in Wales.

Adrian has mixed feelings as he looks back on his international career. "While growing up I was one of thousands of children across Wales whose dream was to become a future Welsh outside half - to follow in the steps of national legends like Cliff Morgan, Barry John or Phil Bennett. I count myself extremely fortunate to have realised that dream.

"The Welsh public has a fanatical obsession with the number ten shirt and it is usually at the number ten's door where either euphoric adulation or the brunt of the criticism is fielded following a Welsh performance. However, despite this emotional roller coaster, I wouldn't have swapped the opportunity to take on that challenge and represent my country as outside half for any other sporting honour.

"I played nine times for Wales, but never played more than two games in a row. This was partly because of changing coaches and perhaps the influence of the media. The great Welsh disasters, 6-63 in Australia and the first ever defeat by Canada, were two games I might have been better to miss.

"I know I did not perform to the best of my ability in the Welsh shirt and did not achieve what I should have, for whatever reason - perhaps all the hype over the number ten shirt. I do feel had I been picked for a run of games I would have done better, but that is just the way it is. I am satisfied that over a number of years, week in, week out - for Neath, Cardiff and Richmond - I played well at club level. But when it comes to international sides, the selectors pick the team and there's nothing you can do.

"I sometimes wonder why God gave me this talent - and there's no doubt my talent came to light on a number of occasions – but never allowed me to perform to the level I know I am capable of. For whatever reason it did not happen. I have no real answers. Having put the effort in for so many years, finally you get the chance and it doesn't happen for you on the day. It's not that I think about it every day and become frustrated, but sometimes looking back, I can't help thinking what might have been."

This chapter was written by Stuart Weir

JOSH DAVIS

RELAYING THE MESSAGE

On August 12, 2000, Josh Davis achieved a goal set over a decade earlier. Swimming at the US Olympic swim trials in Indianapolis, Davis received a standing ovation as he broke Matt Biondi's American 200m freestyle record. He stopped the clock at 1:47.26, shaving 0.46 seconds off the old mark.

Twelve years and four days earlier Davis had been poolside for Biondi's swim. "I was fifteen and had only just started swimming, and my mum bought me a ticket to the Olympic trials in Austin, Texas. Biondi was my idol, and watching him set that record that day, I set myself the goal of one day going that fast."

Davis reached his goal and booked a spot on the US team for the Sydney Olympics, where he would swim even faster. Josh first encountered the Games at twelve. "I remember sitting in my living room watching the men's 4 x 200m freestyle relay and seeing the US men overcome insurmountable odds to win the gold."

From that moment Davis wanted to be an Olympian, but was too busy with other sports to consider training and racing. He had already taken to the water when he moved to a new neighbourhood full of swimmers, but it wasn't until the following year that a friend encouraged him to join an all-year swim club.

"Being a novice," Davis says, "my strokes were not very good. My freestyle and backstroke were ok, but my butterfly was terrible and my breaststroke wasn't even legal. Unfortunately, I inferred from my coach that I should switch sports. After talking with my parents, we decided instead of switching sports to switch coaches. It's amazing what happens with a new coach.

"My new coach taught me all the big and little things it takes to become an elite athlete: technique, streamlining, intensity, strategy, nutrition, flexibility. Sure enough, these things began to work. Soon after, I went from novice to Texas state champion in the 200m free by the time I was fifteen.

"That was the same year I was inspired by Matt Biondi in the 1988 Seoul Olympics. I taped all of his swims and watched them almost every day. I learnt so much from watching the great ones, and then at practice I tried to imitate them."

In 1990, Davis enrolled in the University of Texas and began training under Olympic coach Eddie Reese. In his freshman year, the relay team won the NCAA swimming championships with Davis' help, but with success came excessive celebrations.

"Many athletes pride themselves on training hard," Josh says, "but unfortunately, when the season is over, especially if they win, some pride themselves on partying hard as well. Afraid of being rejected, and lacking in character, I chose to party also. After drinking too much, studying late hours, and training, my body broke down and I became very sick."

After the finals, Davis went home and lay ill in bed for two weeks. "To be stuck in bed for that long made me analyse my life. I thought to myself, 'I have everything society says I'm supposed to have to be happy: my national championship ring, making good grades, my name in the newspaper, and I'm a popular guy on the team. But here I am stuck in bed, can't even move, and I'm completely empty and unsatisfied on the inside."

Josh had been brought up in a Christian family, and knew what the problem was. "God had allowed me to get to a point in my life where he had my attention. I said a simple prayer, just admitting to God that I didn't know what I was doing. I asked him to take control and make me the kind of man he wanted me to be.

"In a way," Davis adds, "Jesus Christ was my new head coach. It's amazing what happens when you get a great coach. I realised I could talk to him anytime and read his message to me in the Bible. For the first time, it was a real and personal relationship. It wasn't a crutch, religion, or an emotional experience; it was a new and real friendship.

"My freshman year I had two new coaches, Eddie Reese and Jesus Christ. I listened to Eddie to train my body, and I listened to Jesus to train my spirit. What God communicated to me through the Bible was that my character is more important than my worldly success. I learnt he loves me so much he doesn't want anything getting in the way of our relationship. I would need to be reminded this truth many times throughout my career but I knew I now had God's direction and peace."

Under the guidance of these two new coaches, Josh competed in the Olympic trials in 1992. "Many consider the trials to be more intense than the Olympics themselves. Every four years there's one night, in a race just over a minute long, that you have to finish first or second. If it's an off day, too bad, better luck four years later. I felt very young, was very nervous, and didn't swim as I had hoped. However, I set a goal that I would be at the 1996 US trials prepared for the pressure and ready to make the Olympic team."

The following year, Davis won his first individual NCAA title, the 200-yard freestyle (scholastic and collegiate meets are measured in yards in the United States), and was a finalist in the 200-yard individual medley and 200-yard butterfly. He also picked up a Pan Pacific title in the 200m.

Josh's success continued. One of the most exciting races of his college career was in his senior year in 1994 when Texas broke the 400-yard relay record, edging out Stanford who led until the last twenty-five yards. Earlier, Josh was beaten in the 200-yard freestyle despite having moved up the rankings from fourth to first.

"It was a time when God was able to teach me some things," he explains. "I finished fifth, though I was ranked number one in the nation. God was more concerned about my character than my aquatic success. It would have been easy to sulk, but I came back and did a lifetime best on the relay by almost a second, swimming 42.1s."

As an American national team member, Davis represented the US in the Pan American Games and at the World Championships in Rome in 1994, where he swam with the relay team that set a new meet record of 3:16.9, barely missing the world record by four-tenths of a second.

Training in 1995 included more yardage and greater intensity. "Coach Reese's philosophy is to do something harder each year to increase your speed. This approach gave me some of my fastest times," says Davis.

That year Josh won his first national titles in the 200m and 400m, and swam what was at that time one of the fastest times in 200m freestyle history (1:48.41) when leading off the 4 x 200m freestyle relay at the World University Games in Fukuoka, Japan. He earned gold in the other two relays and the 400m freestyle, and a bronze in the 100m. He was named team captain and chosen to carry the flag for the US delegation.

1995 was also a great year for Davis personally, marrying his girlfriend of two years in May. Shantel made an impression on Josh when she came to Austin to play volleyball. They wound up spending a lot of time together at Fellowship of Christian Athletes meetings, in church activities and in the athletes' dining hall.

Josh felt the timing was right, even though he faced the pressures of the 1996 Olympic trials in March in Indianapolis. “My marriage was well-established,” says Davis. “I felt making the Olympic team was a realistic goal and I was ranked first in the 200m free at the time. The adrenaline rush, level of excitement and really high stakes are different at the Olympic trials. You get less than two minutes on one night to prove yourself.”

Josh qualified with forty-three other swimmers to represent the United States in Atlanta, earning an individual spot in the 200m freestyle and positions in the 4 x 100m and 4 x 200m relay teams. No one anticipated what this would mean.

“Just to have competed in the Olympics is a tremendous honour,” Davis says. “I realised that honour when I finished seventh in my individual race in the 200m free. At first, I was disappointed because I was concerned about what the media and others would say. But I knew I had done my very best at that moment, and I was extremely proud to have represented my family and country. Besides, seventh in the world is pretty good. Although content, I could never have imagined what God had in store for me in the relays.

“My next event was the 4 x 200m free relay. We were the underdogs and described by the media as lucky to get third. We ended up winning by a landslide. Receiving that gold medal and singing our national anthem was almost as good as marrying Shantel.

“After that was the 4 x 100m free relay. The pressure was amazing. America had never lost this relay in Olympic history, and now the Russians had their fastest relay ever assembled ready to break our streak. We came from behind and beat them, and busted the Olympic record in the process. I had now received a second gold medal."

The sprint relay was also significant because it decided who would race in the medley relay. Gary Hall Jr would anchor the relay having recorded what was then the fastest ever split, in 47.4 seconds, and the next fastest would anchor the morning preliminary relay. If the final relay wins, both are awarded gold medals.

Davis' split of 49.0 was just enough, edging out teammate Brad Schumacher by one-hundredth of a second. "The final relay easily won the gold medal," Josh remembers, "breaking the world record by an astonishing two seconds. I was awarded my third gold medal. I had the great blessing of being the only male in any sport at the 1996 Olympic Games to get three gold medals."

Despite his success, celebrity pressures far from bombarded Davis. "Not everyone notices when relays win gold," he says. "Hardly anyone recognises me in Austin. However, I was hailed an immediate hero in my hometown, San Antonio." That's where the state-of-the-art Josh Davis Aquatic Center now honours his accomplishments.

In 1997, Josh and Shantel had their first son, Caleb, and have since added a daughter, Abby, and another boy just days before the Sydney Olympics, Luke. The adjustments to marriage and parenthood have not always been easy. Josh knows his wife understands the hard work and need for the rigorous training schedule he still maintains but is sensitive to her needs too, and regards his work as a parent as the hardest and most important task he has.

"I don't think I could reach my full potential as a swimmer if I didn't have my wife and kids," Davis adds. "They are my main source of motivation when I am training and going through pain barriers. They are a constant source of joy in good times and bad. When I have problems or fears, they all seem to vanish when my son or daughter runs into my arms with a big smile."

Josh's success in the pool continued with his record-breaking swim at the 2000 US Olympic trials. At the Sydney Games, Davis produced the swim of his life but could only add two silver medals to his tally, in the 4 x 200m and 4 x 100m relays.

In the 200m semi-final, Josh lowered the American record to 1:47.06, but the race he'll always remember from the Sydney Olympics is the final against Ian Thorpe, Pieter van den Hoogenband and Massimiliano Rosolino, where he swam 1:46.73.

"Fourteen years of training culminating in just one minute and forty-six seconds. So many thoughts ran through my mind. I asked for God's grace, wisdom, and strength. Purposefully, I gave my doubts, fear, and worries to him, and renewed my mind with God's truth. My prayer was that I would swim all-out to the best of my ability and trust him with the results - to actually give my swim to him as my spiritual act of worship.

"As the eight finalists gathered in the Ready Room we knew it would be a four-man race: Ian the Aussie favourite, Pieter the flying Dutchman, Massi the fast Italian, and me. We nodded to each other communicating without words that we respected each other - and may the best man win. We also knew one of us would not get a medal.

"As we filed into the darkened hallway before marching onto the brightly lit pool deck, all I could see were the huge shoulders of Ian in front of me. At six-foot-five, 220 lbs., unbeaten in years, world record holder, and hometown hero, he was an intimidating opponent. The two-minute wait to march out seemed more like two hours. I quickly prayed against thoughts of fear, resting in God's provision. Like so many times before, I knew he would give me what I needed when I needed it, and probably not a second too soon. Next the inescapable moment: the monotone voice echoed throughout the venue, 'Please welcome the finalists in the men's 200m freestyle.' As we walked out from under the awning, a wave of lights and noise from 18,000 cheering fans greeted us. The deafening crowd had been anticipating this race for days and I couldn't help but smile and embrace that amazing moment.

"Right before the official called us to the blocks I said one last prayer: 'Lord help me to go all out for you and with you, regardless of time or place. Thank you for being with me. Let's have some fun.' In just a few seconds the amazingly loud crowd came to a complete silence. 'Swimmers take your mark.' Thirty thousand miles of training over the last fourteen years were now coming down to one moment in time.

"Bang! The starter's gun released me into the water to race just 200m. I felt great the whole way. I was first at the 50m mark, tied for second at the 100m, third at the 150m. In the final 10m all of us put our heads down and reached for the wall. Being human I looked immediately to what my place was: next to my name was a number four. The Dutchman had won, with the Aussie second, the Italian, and then me. I then looked at my time and saw I had busted my own American record by a good margin, it was my lifetime best time and would have won any of the previous Olympics. I realised my prayer had been answered. God was with me during the race so I could swim my best, and was with me now. God had been glorified, and I had swam faster than I had ever swam before. I was a part of the greatest 200m freestyle race of all time.

"After the race I was on a natural physical high for just having raced well, and on a supernatural high because God answered my prayers. But my Olympic moment wouldn't be complete without seeing my loved ones who came to cheer me on. While making my way to the dressing room it began to hit me what had just happened. I couldn't hold back the intense emotions that rose up. I trained so hard for so long only to miss an individual medal by one-tenth of a second.

"Although I know it's just a piece of metal, I could not separate my emotions from the reality of having sacrificed so much. I gave it my all daily for four years and then I gave it my all one last time in the Olympic final. The mix of emotions when it was all done was overwhelming. That's the beauty of a relationship with God: we can be totally human, vulnerable, and honest. Even though my feelings didn't line up with God's truth at that moment, I could still trust him.

"When I saw my parents I burst into tears. They hugged me and we were laughing and crying all at the same time. They were so proud of me. They kept telling me over and over how proud, pleased, and surprised they were at how fast I swam, and what a great race it was. In my final embrace with my Dad I held him tighter and longer than normal and just wept. Trying to talk through the tears I whispered in his ear, 'Dad, I hope I made you proud.' Like always he quickly said, 'Of course I'm always so proud of you.' I knew it and I've always known it, but it felt so good to hear it. Whether you're eight, eighteen, or twenty-eight, you need to know you're unconditionally loved. My parents provide so much freedom to excel. They do such a good job of being visible examples and reminders of God's invisible love.

"Greater than winning Olympic medals was hearing my Dad say, 'Well done, I'm so proud of you.' How much greater will the culmination of our existence be when we hear our perfect heavenly father say, 'Well done, my good and faithful servant.'

Davis hopes to compete until the 2008 Olympics, basing his life on a simple philosophy. "What I do has worked for centuries," he says. "I have my priorities in order: God, family and then vocation."

This chapter was written with the help of Jennie Chandler

JOE DELOACH

WHEN THE GAMES ARE OVER

Joe DeLoach is one of the greatest athletes of all time, yet most people have never heard of him. He is an Olympic champion and record holder, yet only scratched the surface of his potential. Among those who know sprinting, no praise is too high for the Texan.

Nine-time Olympic gold medallist, Carl Lewis says, "Joe DeLoach was one of the most talented athletes I have ever seen. He easily had the talent to run as fast as anybody. I don't think there is any question he could have done it." Another former 100m world record holder, Leroy Burrell adds, "Joe is one of the most talented, naturally gifted, effortless runners there has ever been."

Joe Douglas, the man behind the Santa Monica Track Club, says, "The only person in the world who could touch Joe was Carl Lewis. Joe could have won another Olympics. Nobody else could have touched him; he was too good. His talent was astronomical." DeLoach's coach at the University of Houston, Tom Tellez, concludes, "Joe could have been the best of all time, he definitely had the potential... he could have run very close to nine-flat."

DeLoach was born in the small town of Bay City, Texas, in 1967 – the youngest of fourteen siblings. Before Joe even reached his teens, he knew he was fast. His father was also fast runner and they often raced. The son vividly remembers the first time he won. "My family used to visit my oldest sister, JoAnne, about once a year around Thanksgiving," he says. "Everyone loved going to JoAnne's. She was like a mother to me. JoAnne actually had two children who were older than me, so she was literally old enough to be my mother. Every time a few of us kids had to stay home because they couldn't fit everyone in the car. I watched for years as the older kids stayed behind, and now it was my turn.

"I cried and whined. They got in the car and were pulling off, and I began shouting obscenities towards them. My dad slammed on the brakes. I saw those red brake lights; my eyes got so big. I knew I was in trouble. He opened the door and was out. I was standing at the back of the car. When I saw my dad get out, I started running. My dad started running as hard as he could. I could hear him behind me.

"That day my dad never caught me, I had that much speed. I remember feeling a sense of joy I had outrun my dad, but on the other hand I knew I had to come back home eventually, and I knew I was going to get a whooping."

At Bay City High School, DeLoach began revealing his potential under the guidance of coach Marshall Brown. Competing in the Texas state championships at sixteen, he easily won the 200m title in 20.76 seconds, but in the 100m left the crowd in shock, becoming the champion in 10.0 seconds.

Unfortunately the wind-reading was deemed too high, keeping him from claiming the world high school record of 10.16 seconds. The overall world record belonged to Calvin Smith with 9.93 seconds.

After the state meet, DeLoach focused his attentions on the junior nationals in Los Angeles where he again won the sprint double. On the back of these performances he qualified for the Junior Olympics in the Bahamas. Following in Carl Lewis' footsteps set down four years earlier, Joe again won the 100m and 200m, and also anchored the 4 x 100m relay to victory to become the first person ever to win three gold medals at the same Junior Olympics.

DeLoach's form continued throughout the rest of high school and into college at the University of Houston. In Houston, Joe began to train with the likes of Carl Lewis. "I knew I was in a very special situation," he says, "a situation many sprinters aspired to be in, to be training with the greatest of them all."

Joe and Carl raced each other competitively for the first time at the Texas Southern University (TSU) Relays in March 1986. "I was really excited about that race," DeLoach says. "There were so many people there it was powerful. Even though it was cold, it was an electrifying feeling as we prepared. This was the biggest race of my life, racing against my mentor for the first time.

"I had to run my best race because Carl always puts on a good performance. I knew if I did my best it would show me how much work I had ahead of me before I could get to Carl's level."

To the shock of everyone, Joe won. "When I crossed the finish line ahead of Carl in the 100m, I had no idea. I was so focused for this race I didn't see him. I crossed the finish line and then looked to the side and saw Carl cross after me. I was stunned."

Despite an injury hurdle when DeLoach pulled his hamstring in the collegiate national 100m final, he continued to develop, now fixing his eyes on Olympic glory in Seoul in 1988. Unfortunately, his dreams for the 100m soon ended at the Olympic trials, finishing fifth in the final. Joe's time was a wind-assisted 9.90 seconds. Seven runners in that race broke the ten-second barrier, more than in any other 100m race ever. Only four-hundredths of a second separated Joe in fifth and Dennis Mitchell in second.

"Not only was this loss going through my mind," DeLoach says, "but I didn't have many days left before the 200m. There was total disappointment, but it gave me motivation. I realised I couldn't wait another four years, I had to make it happen now. Now was the time for me to do it. Now was my moment."

Despite his failure in the 100m, DeLoach's goal to become an Olympic champion was unshaken. In the 200m final he clocked 19.96 seconds to win and beat Lewis. This convinced him he was ready.

"When I beat Carl it told me I was in the company of the great. It let me know I was right where I needed to be. We have to position ourselves for success, and that race positioned me for my final challenge: the Olympic Games. Carl was the measuring rod for any sprinter's success at that time, crossing the finish line before him told me I was right where I needed to be."

Finally, DeLoach's moment to become a champion arrived. Standing in lane six in the 200m Olympic final - his friend, training partner and now main rival three lanes over on the inside – he got down in his blocks and waited for the gun.

"When I heard the gun fire I was still nervous," DeLoach says, "but I reached down with everything in me and began to drive like crazy. When I drove out of those blocks, I put forth all the energy I had. When I finally came up I was midway to the turn and that was the first time I saw Carl leading me. I had already made up the stagger on everyone else, but not Carl. I was comfortable in my race. I quickly glanced at the crowd. I could see them in my peripheral vision. Then I looked to the left and saw Carl ahead of me.

"I didn't panic. That's when all the training began to kick in. I could hear echoing in my mind: relax, run your own race, he'll come back to you. If I had thought about it being Carl Lewis out there I probably would have panicked, but in that race Carl was just like everyone else. He was just another athlete. He got out of the blocks well, ran a great turn and was in front of me.

"I was relaxed. I charged off the turn and saw Carl come towards me. I was even more confident. I just stayed in my rhythm. The other runners were a few meters behind us, I couldn't feel any pressure from them. I was thinking, 'Just relax Joe.'

"I went through every swing of my arms, every lift of my legs, with total relaxation. I was in the zone. I was in my own world. After I catapulted off the turn I saw Carl one last time. I totally relaxed and executed everything I was supposed to.

"In the last five meters of the race I finally caught Carl. I could see Carl in my peripheral vision, almost like a shadow to my left. I knew I could win the race. I put forth a last surge to go even faster, to dig even deeper, and as I hit the finish line I leaned and turned my head slightly to the left. When I leaned I saw my torso ahead of his over the finish line. I won it. I did it. I had won the gold."

As well as taking the gold medal from Carl, DeLoach took his Olympic record. "I didn't care what I ran," he says, "I just wanted to win the gold. But when I saw the time was 19.75 seconds, I knew it was a fast race. I had no idea it was an American and Olympic record until they announced it. The records just made it that much more special."

With a gold medal around his neck, Joe believed he was set for success. But at a low-key meet in the Bahamas in 1989, he again twitched his hamstring. The following year the problem worsened, DeLoach resorting to surgery for an answer.

In late 1990, the sprinter returned to training and qualified for the follow year's national championships. Cruising through the rounds of the 200m, DeLoach beat Mike Marsh in the semifinals in 20.12 seconds. "I had climbed a mountain getting through surgery, and now I was again at my peak. Going into the final everyone was talking about me again. I had to turn it on. I was ready both mentally and physically.

"I was leading coming out of the turn, but again I pulled up injured. That was a world championship year and I really needed to make it. I was heart broken. I tried so hard. I did so much to come back. I didn't see how I could go on. I knew the Olympics were the following year and I had to prepare myself, but I was the most heart broken I had ever felt."

Joe's disappointments on the track made him question his faith in God. "My faith became an issue," he says. "Where is God when it really matters? Where is God when it hurts? I was hurting. I was desperate. I needed a God who answered prayer, and in the way I wanted him to. I wanted to run and not get injured. That's all I asked of God. I said, 'I'll do the rest. You just let me run and not get injured.'

"Every time I got injured, I felt God let me down. He didn't keep his end of the bargain. He didn't do what he was supposed to do. After all, he was God. He could do all things. I questioned my faith. God seemed to be a dispassionate onlooker who wasn't involved in the meaningful affairs of people's lives. Track and field was meaningful to me and he hadn't done a thing to help. I developed the attitude that I was saved and would go to heaven, but that God didn't care about the everyday issues of our lives."

Despite his doubts, DeLoach decided to go to a healing service held by Benny Hinn. "He was holding a meeting in Oklahoma," Joe remembers. "I believed God would heal me. It was a nine-hour drive to Tulsa, but I decided to do it. I was excited. I got to the meeting and when he started calling people who needed healing I went down. I walked up on the stage, I didn't know what was going to happen to me, but I needed to be healed. I crossed the stage; Benny Hinn put a microphone in my hand and asked me what was going on. I told him and he prayed for me. I believed I was healed."

What DeLoach believed was wrong. Two weeks before the 1992 Olympic trials his body again gave way. "My leg felt tight and uncomfortable, but I told myself I was healed. Carl, Mike Marsh and I were practicing the 200m. We were supposed to be running about eighty-percent around the turn, but I needed to see what my legs could endure. I pushed myself a little harder, and when I did I pulled my quad. I did so much work on the back of my leg it put pressure on the front. My quad detached from my knee.

"I was humiliated. I thought it was bad at the nationals, but at least I walked off the track then. Now I lay on the track, looked up at the heavens and said, 'Why!' I knew instantly my hopes of making Barcelona were shattered.

"First I believed God didn't care, then I believed he would heal me, and then I ripped my quad to shreds before the Olympic trials. Immediately I began questioning again. Where is God when it hurts?"

During these struggles, DeLoach sat through the Barcelona Olympics. "It was so frustrating I could hardly stand it. In 1988, I was part of the Olympics and even won gold. Now I was just a spectator. There were certain moments too overwhelming for me.

"I sat at home on my couch watching the Opening Ceremony, and when they got to the American athletes I saw all the guys I knew. They were happy, rejoicing, jumping up and down. Tears were rolling down my face. I had to get up and leave. I was really angry with God.

"When the 100m and the 200m came on, I tried to watch. I saw Mike Marsh getting ready for the 200m. I was happy because I knew Mike personally, but I also felt I was supposed to be there. Watching was almost an out-of-body experience. I didn't belong in my living room, I belonged out there on the track.

"As much as I had experienced my dreams come to pass, this was a nightmare. I was devastated. I tried to be excited with my family, they knew Mike and Carl and those guys. I tried to be excited, but I had to leave. I went straight to my room, laid facedown and cried.

"I couldn't believe my dreams were passing me by. I asked God why he was allowing it to happen. I began questioning him. It was terrible. I didn't think I would live beyond those moments. I couldn't wait for the Games to finish. Every day that I woke up and the Games were still on, there was pain and frustration. It would never leave. It haunted me. It was all I could think about. As powerful as I had been in winning the gold medal, there was nothing I could do to change what I was experiencing. It was the most helpless feeling anybody could have."

While Joe was at the height of his despair, a preacher at church spoke on What happens if the miracle doesn't come? "That was my life," DeLoach says. "I had been waiting on a miracle for the past four years, and the miracle didn't come. The preacher said everybody wasn't going to get the resolution they wanted for every situation. What God promises is that he will not let us be tempted beyond what we can bear. You've got to be prepared to deal with things. You've got to be prepared to face the realities of life. There are some things you can't control. That was the hardest thing for me. I was a world-class athlete, someone who made it to the top of the mountain, who conquered life; I thought there was nothing I couldn't do. I was living with that in my mind, but came to the conclusion there were some things I had no control over. I had to accept it.

"I also realised what a wretched man I was. When it came down to it, I didn't deserve anything from God. I deserved hell but was given grace, God's unmerited favour. I realised how selfish I had been in my life, how I wanted God to be my cosmic errand boy. I wanted to push his sovereign buttons, and receive from his glorious vending machine whatever it was that suited my needs."

Joe decided to accept Jesus Christ not only as the saviour of his life but also as his lord. "It changed me," he says. "I became less presumptuous and more grateful for every moment I have, for everything I can accomplish, for every breath God has given me, for life."

In 1994, DeLoach returned to the track but was unable to reach the levels he once took for granted. The strains of constant disappointments took a heavy toll on Joe and his wife, Melony. But as they worked through the turmoil, it strengthened their relationships with each other and with God.

"I am a sinner and have fallen short of his standards," Joe says. "I am vulnerable to evil. I need to depend on God. Even after I have done my best, I still fall short of what it takes to please God. I am a man whose life is filled with spots and blemishes, but when I was in the darkest moment of my life I realised God could forgive me, no matter what I did.

"The times I was most alone helped me understand what it means to have God in your life. God is a friend like no other. When I was filled with solitude and loneliness, I didn't think anyone could understand what happened in that moment, but God proved to me he could. That is when I understood that a person's greatest need is a relationship with the only and true, almighty God. He is our maker; he understands us. God understands and forgives.

"On the cross, Jesus died and took my sins so I could be forgiven. We are made righteous not because of what we have done, but because of what Jesus did. We are justified through what he accomplished, not through our accomplishments. Jesus' death and resurrection is my salvation, and also my motivation for wanting to live a life pleasing to God.

"I trained for years to run 19.75 seconds. That's the kind of commitment we need to show God. When you understand what the cross means, you realise God has a right to expect a world-class lifestyle, a world-class effort. The same cross that lets us understand Christ died for us so we can have a relationship with God, also calls us to excellence.

"When you meet Jesus it causes a drastic change in your life. Meeting Jesus is about change, a change in life and a change in perspective. There are too many people who say they are Christians, but are comfortable in this world. We must strive to live a life reflecting the grace God shows us.

"My relationship with God hasn't been perfect, but God is continuing to strengthen my faith and mould me into the person he wants me to be. Throughout my life I have strived for treasure that lasts only for this lifetime, but now I'm striving for a far more valuable treasure. I'm now living my life for God, seeking to be the husband, father and ambassador he wants me to be.

"It hurts to know I could have been one of the greatest sprinters of all time but failed to reach my full potential. It still hurts now, but I am no longer bitter at God for what I didn't receive. Instead I am thankful for the blessings he chose to give me, especially my relationship with him and my loving family."

JONATHAN EDWARDS

LEAP OF FAITH

On June 7, 1995 in Gothenburg, Sweden, Jonathan Edwards brought the athletics world to a standstill. Competing in the World Championships, he shattered his own triple jump world record of 17.98m twice. No sooner had he jumped 18.16m than he bettered it with a leap of 18.29m - a distance unlikely to be beaten for a very long time.

The *Daily Mail* newspaper in England filled its back page with the words: "Three steps to heaven", describing Edward's effort as "leaving everyone punch drunk with disbelief."

Journalist Mike Rowbottom wrote: "After the first jump, Edwards was bewildered for a moment, but he had his head in his hands. His second jump was pure joy. As he stood up, he simply smiled widely with the enjoyment of the moment, basking in the afternoon sunshine and the tumultuous applause."

Edwards' leaps were not a complete shock to those who had been following his progress. At the European Cup he recorded wind assisted clearances of 18.43m and 18.39m, and three weeks later broke Willie Banks' world record by one centimetre with a 17.98m jump in Salamanca, Spain.

That year was an amazing time for Edwards and his athletics career. In fourteen competitions, he won fourteen times, setting five British records and three world records, and won the World Championship gold medal.

"At the World Championships," he remembers, "there was obviously a lot of expectation on me - people thought I might break the world record, and I did break it in the first round. I was the first person to jump over eighteen-metres legally. Then in the second round I broke it again and jumped over sixty-feet. It was just an incredible day, to go through two barriers - both the metric and the imperial - in twenty-minutes was too much for me to take in.

"It was so easy that year, I thought I would again challenge it myself, but even I've not come close. It makes me appreciate that it is a strong world record. It's quite a humbling experience, and slightly surreal, that no one has ever jumped further than me and no one has ever really even got close."

Modest and unassuming, Edwards is an unlikely superstar. His early life was spent in a warm Christian environment. At home there was love and discipline. He learnt amongst other things that putting God first required sacrifice. For instance, Sunday was regarded as a special day. At school and college, Jonathan never did academic work on a Sunday. It was a day for church, rest, writing letters, reading books and being with the family. To the Edwards family, their faith and family were priorities and they protected them in part by keeping Sunday special.

Jonathan loved all sport at school, and played most of them with skill. By 1984, he was excelling in the triple jump and won his first major title, taking the English Schools gold. But to Edwards, the triple jump was still just a hobby and he would never compete on Sundays - this initially more newsworthy than his performances.

As Edwards continued to improve, he qualified for the 1988 Seoul Olympics. He loved being part of the British team, soaking up the atmosphere. It was also an encouraging time for him as a Christian, spending time with other Christians from around the world, sharing their faith, reading the Bible, singing and praying.

Reflecting on the Games, Jonathan adds, "The Olympics are often used to highlight the need for peace between humans, along with human achievement. But the world's greatest need is to find peace with God and this has been made possible by the achievements of one man - Jesus Christ."

Jonathan can't remember a time when he was not a Christian. He saw the reality of God in his parents' lives, and his own faith gradually matured. Only when he left home for university did he really stand out as a believer. "I have never not known God," he says, "although I realise I haven't always been a Christian. God has always been there."

Edwards' breakthrough spiritually came when his father pestered him to use his God-given talent as a triple jumper. "I came to see that my father was right," Jonathan says, "and that a Christian sportsman would have an opportunity to share his faith. As believers, we are all ambassadors for Christ and that is what I was being called to be. I began to see my sport in the context of my faith. I thought that since God had given me this ability, he would want me to use it."

Edwards is clear about what he believes. "All of us are sinful and are separated from God - we can do nothing about that. But of his own will God sent his son, Jesus, to die on the cross for our sins and rise again. By having faith in him, we can be reconciled to God. In response to that gift, we are to give our lives to God."

Reading the Bible is an essential part of his life: "The Bible is God's word to me - to all of us - to what my attitudes, my actions and the way I live my life should be. It's God's primary way of speaking to me. From the Bible, I have acquired the basic philosophy for what I try to do - to glorify God through every aspect of my life."

Back in 1988, as a part-time athlete, Jonathan's "never on a Sunday" policy was fine, but over the next few years athletics was to turn his life upside down. It wasn't until 1993, when he left his job at a genetics laboratory to become a full-time athlete, he decided to compete on Sundays.

In 1989, Edwards became Britain's number one triple jumper, and the following year took silver at the Commonwealth Games in Auckland. Soon he was thinking seriously of a medal at the 1992 Barcelona Olympics. In fact, his second Olympics turned into a nightmare. Although he had been consistently jumping around seventeen-metres, he failed to even reach sixteen and did not qualify for the final. He was totally shattered by the experience.

"It was probably the worst period of my life," he says. "I was absolutely devastated. All my hopes and dreams had been blown out of the water. I remember thinking: 'This is just a dream, it can't have happened.' It was awful. I was taken to depths I had not known previously."

The experience in Spain led Jonathan to consider his entire life. Should he continue in athletics? Did God have a purpose in his athletics? Was he really glorifying God, win or lose? Was God central in his life? He had always felt triple jumping was integral to him as a person - a gift from God, even though he does not think that triple jumping in itself glorifies God. Although, as Edwards points out, "the fact that a human being can jump 18.29m is testimony to what a great God we serve."

As he looks back on 1992 and other hard times, he sees the setbacks and difficulties as vital in helping lay a foundation for what was ahead. The world record-holder loves jumping a long way, and loves winning, but also knows his attitude and perspective are what count.

Edwards' performances began to pick up after 1992. He won bronze at the World Championships in 1993 and silver at the Commonwealth Games in Vancouver the following year. By 1995 he was a world-class athlete, but nobody could have predicted what was to happen that year. Even he cannot explain it. "I was running faster, I was stronger, I improved my technique - but it still did not add up. Obviously, I was not in touch with my potential. I look back and shake my head."

The eighteen-metre mark had been the four-minute-mile of triple jumping. It was the barrier no one could cross. Triple jumpers went seventeen-metres, not eighteen - never. Jonathan didn't just break the barrier, he smashed it twice in the blink of an eye. Suddenly, he was rich and recognised. Award followed award.

"I jumped three times into a sandpit and suddenly I was famous," commented the bemused champion. When he became the BBC Sports Personality of the Year in December 1995, he stammered, "Thank you very much. I'm afraid I've never really been able to watch this program because I've always been at church."

Life in Newcastle with his wife, Alison, and their two boys was transformed. A large house took the place of their two bedroom flat, a Mercedes sat on the forecourt, and a secretary was employed. "There was a lot more money available to me than there had been before," Edwards explains. "That is difficult. The Bibles talks about the love of money being the root of all evil. I am under no illusions. I have the same evil desires inside everyone has. The difference is that I also have God's Holy Spirit inside me to help overcome them. I certainly feel, having had disaster as well as incredible success, that the latter represents the biggest threat to my walk with God."

The celebrity status Edwards attained in 1995 placed many pressures on him. "I've never been so scared in my life," he admitted before the 1996 Atlanta Olympics. "Coping away from the track has been as tough as competing on it."

Jonathan only managed silver despite being the favourite, ending his twenty-four meet unbeaten run. He lost to American Kenny Harrison, who jumped 18.09m to better Edwards' 17.88m. Harrison's jump remains the only time someone other than Edwards has broken the eighteen-metre barrier.

Again in 1997 at the World Championships, he was beaten into second place, this time hampered by an injury to his left heel. After the jump, Edwards' said, "I didn't do myself justice. I fought hard, but it just wasn't there. I didn't have my normal rhythm."

In 1998, Edwards' form returned. At the European Championships in Budapest in August, he won the gold medal with a championship record of 17.99m, the fifth longest jump of all time. For his efforts, the Briton was honoured as European Athlete of the Year. Unfortunately as Edwards was landing in the pit in Hungary he injured his foot, forcing him to have an operation and withdraw from the World Cup in Johannesburg and the Commonwealth Games in Kuala Lumpur. But the athlete was soon back to his very best with a gold medal at the Goodwill Games later that year in New York. In Seville in 1999, he added another World Championship bronze. Since 1995, Edwards had made four of the five longest leaps of all time, but still one prize eluded him.

Before the 2000 Sydney Olympics, he declared, "These will be my last Olympics and my heart is set on winning the gold medal." Edwards nearly didn't make the Games, his mother-in-law who had been sick for a year with cancer dying within days of the opening ceremony. But, with his wife's blessing, he booked his flight to Sydney.

Over one-hundred-and-ten-thousand fans packed the Olympic Stadium, watching Edwards overcome the bedlam of the moment to jump 17.71m, a distance no one else could better. "I was very nervous," he said afterwards. "There were constant disruptions with medal ceremonies and other races going on. I thought my best chance of winning would be in Atlanta. Now here I am in Sydney four years later, thirty-four years-old and winning the gold medal. I still can't really put together what I've done.

"To win gold at the Olympic Games caps my career," he adds. "I have always had the ability to win an Olympic gold medal and I truly believe God wanted me to. I thank God for his mercy and the fact he's given me the ability to do this, and now I am satisfied."

More viewers were watching Edwards in the stands and on television than on any night in Olympic history, as he completed his best jump since 1995. "My world record five years ago put pressure on me to perform at major meets, and up to now I haven't delivered," he said. "I dedicate this win to my wife for all she has put up with over the past few years and I am proud to say I am taking home this medal to show my sons."

Despite having achieved this crowning triumph, and advancing in years, the thirty-five year-old proved he was still the man to beat at the 2001 World Championships. Competing in Edmonton, Canada, Edwards seized gold with a leap of 17.92m – his biggest jump in three years and the ninth longest of all time.

"It felt great, and I felt I had more in me. If I had been able to attack the board unhindered, I think I might have been able to jump further," the champion said. "It's a pity. I'm thirty-five now and there might not be many more days like this left in my career. I can go on, but I just don't know how much longer for. I just enjoy triple jumping."

This chapter was written with Andrew Wingfield-Digby

NICK FARR-JONES

O CAPTAIN, MY CAPTAIN

On August 21, 1993, the international rugby career of Nick Farr-Jones came to an end with a series winning nineteen-twelve victory over South Africa. To the standing ovation of the Sydney Football Stadium crowd and his fellow players, Nick farewelled the game.

In his ten seasons with the Australian Wallabies the halfback come a long way, notching up sixty-three test appearances – thirty-six times leading his country out as captain. Despite this glory, Nick Farr-Jones' rugby beginnings were not as auspicious as its conclusion.

As a schoolboy at Newington College in Sydney's inner west, Nick was commendable in just about every sport he tried - captaining his teams in rugby, athletics, swimming and tennis. Amid all this sporting success he experienced the disappointment of failing to make the First XV rugby side.

Continuing to Sydney University to study law, Nick joined their well-established rugby club and began making up for the previous year's disappointment. After the trial matches, the coach gathered all the under-twenty-one-year-old players and read the team for the First Colts: "...Halfback: Nick Farr-Jones..."

"When I didn't make the Firsts at school," Nick remembers, "I started wondering if I was already turning into one of those schoolboy athletes who never do anything once they get older, so I was delighted to climb back into a Firsts side."

Nick was integral to the First Colts who won the premiership that year and as a result was promoted to the First Grade side the following season. Over the next couple of years, Uni didn't have the most successful time and in 1983 were relegated to the Second Division. This was a disaster for the club and a major hurdle in Farr-Jones' rugby career. He had as much chance of being selected for representative honours from a Second Division club as when he was at school - almost none.

Despite not being one of the higher ranking halfbacks, Nick was selected for the Sydney tour to Europe in 1984 after a selector saw him play in the combined Second Division side. That year Nick also donned his first green and gold jersey playing for the Australian Universities team during a five week European tour. But the best was yet to come.

In May 1984, Australian rugby coach, Alan Jones, announced the new look Wallaby squad for the season: "...Nick Farr-Jones..." The young sportsman was one step closer to his dream, and on the following Fijian tour debuted with a Man-of-the-Match performance against the Eastern Selection. Farr-Jones' first test cap didn't come until the first game of the famous 1984 Grand Slam tour, playing against England. Over the following ten years Nick's rugby career unfolded.

The 1984 Wallabies won every match of the tour, beating England, Ireland, Wales and Scotland. Nick played in every test and also scored his first *test* try in the victory over Scotland.

Farr-Jones established himself within the Wallabies with a bang. Over the next two seasons he played in all twelve *tests*, scoring four tries and contributing to victories over Canada, Fiji, Italy, France, Argentina and New Zealand. The highlight of these years was the series victory over the All Blacks, recapturing the Bledisloe Cup. The *Australian* newspaper summed up: "Nick Farr-Jones heads our rugby honour roll for '86, and can rightfully lay claim to being the world's best halfback."

In 1987, Farr-Jones got his first taste of representative captaincy when he was named as head of the New South Wales side, displacing Wallaby great, Simon Poidevin. The coach at the time, Paul Dalton, explains: "I always saw Farr-Jones as a natural leader. He was the brain, the architect; he could read a game, decide what had to be done and have the others follow. He was already doing that from his position at halfback, but I wanted him to have full authority, to be captain."

Nick's international captaincy didn't come until 1988, after a year in which the Wallabies lost five straight games and Alan Jones was dumped as coach, replaced by Bob Dwyer. Legend has it that Dwyer, who coached Australia immediately before Jones, began the first Wallaby training session with the words: "Now, as I was saying before I was so rudely interrupted..."

Despite uncertainty surrounding the appointment of Farr-Jones as captain, history has vindicated Dwyer's decision. Under Farr-Jones' captaincy the Wallabies reached the pinnacle of world rugby, even though it took a couple years to get there, losing to New Zealand and England in 1988 and the British Lions in 1989. In all, the Wallabies won only five of their thirteen matches in those two years.

In 1990, the Wallabies brought the All Blacks' four year, twenty-three-game winning streak to an end with a twenty-one to nine win on New Zealand soil, in the third Bledisloe Cup test. The local *Otago Times* wrote: "The greatest off all was Nick Farr-Jones, their captain. The great captains, the great halfbacks, have vision, and that is what Farr-Jones displayed in the Wellington wind and rain. He saw the ground as a chessboard. He made all the right moves and pulled the right strings as he urged even more from his men." Australia won the last test for 1990 and was ready for the main challenge in 1991, the Rugby World Cup.

In the warm-up to the World Cup, the Wallabies knocked over Wales, England and New Zealand, but the real event didn't start until later that year. The Australians made it through to the quarterfinals of the Rugby World Cup, with only a knee injury to Farr-Jones slowing them down. This injury also caused him to leave the field early in the quarterfinal against Ireland. Sitting on the sidelines, Nick watched his team come from behind to score in the dying moments and win nineteen-eighteen. In the semifinal, the Wallabies had an extraordinary sixteen to six victory over the All Blacks - New Zealand losing for only the third time since 1987. Australia had earned their way into the 1991 Rugby World Cup final.

On the first Saturday afternoon in November, Australian rugby was about to have a moment. Twickenham in London was packed with 60,000 fans, hundreds of millions more watching around the world. The players from Australia and England assembled on the ground and, after meeting Queen Elizabeth II, joined in the singing of their national anthems. Eighty minutes after the first whistle blew, the Wallabies had won, twelve-six. Amid hugs and cheers, Nick ascended the stairs to the Queen to receive the William Webb Ellis trophy. The Australians were world champions.

Farr-Jones and the other players were bombarded with accolades from all sources. English magazine *Rugby News* wrote: "The Wallabies' triumph proves conclusively that nice guys can win. The courtesy and manners shown by men like Bob Dwyer and his captain Nick Farr-Jones were exemplary. These two and their colleagues were the finest ambassadors for their country. Their rugby matched them, the game and its much cherished reputation was in excellent hands." Upon returning to Sydney, the city held a tickertape parade to honour the team and at its conclusion the Lord Mayor presented the captain with the Key to the City.

After eight years of international rugby only one thing remained that Farr-Jones had not achieved, and his opportunity to do so came a year later in 1992. Twenty-three years after their last meeting, due to their opponent's suspension from international sport because of apartheid, Australia played South Africa. Only a win over the Springboks would establish Australia as the unquestioned world champions. South Africa was sure it would be victorious, but at fulltime the scoreboard read twenty-six to three in Australia's favour, the biggest loss the Springboks had suffered in one-hundred years.

The All Blacks were also in South Africa to play the home side, seeking to restore their pride after losing the Bledisloe Cup. Several kiwi supporters stayed in the same hotel as the Wallabies and enjoyed sitting at the bar loudly pondering how Australia could have been so lucky as to beat New Zealand.

Farr-Jones and teammate Tony Daly thought of a way to shut them up. Summoning the young hotel page, who carried a large blackboard with messages on it, they told him what to do. He changed his board and headed to the All Black supporters. Ringing his bell and waving the blackboard, he asked if anyone knew where Lord Bledisloe or Mr William Webb Ellis were. On cue the Wallabies shouted, "They're over here! We've got them both!"

After the South African victory, Nick Farr-Jones had achieved all there was to achieve in rugby. One year later, he played his last game at the Sydney Football Stadium, leaving victoriously in front of his home crowd.

Over his career, Farr-Jones had some amazing experiences: beating every major rugby playing nation, winning the World Cup and the Bledisloe Cup, and meeting the Queen and Nelson Mandela. Despite these amazing experiences, he rates none as being more amazing than what happened when he was sixteen.

"I was at the local pizza shop chasing a couple of ladies after the Cronulla Leagues Club closed and it so happened they were Christian girls. The way I could see them again was by going to church. They invited me along and I started to go. I heard the gospel, and when you hear the gospel preached in a simple way it's pretty hard not to accept, and for the first time I heard the gospel preached. I thought, 'This is irrefutable!' - and not only hearing the gospel, but seeing the way the Spirit moved among these people. There was something that distinguished them from the people I was mixing with at the Leagues Club, and I wanted a bit of that."

Over time, Nick became more involved with his new friends and his commitment to follow Christ began to impact on his life, most noticeably by calming his temper. Nick's brother, Simon, remembers one time he went to the local pub for a few beers with Nick and some of his friends. "We were sitting at a table having a beer and these guys were sitting next to us drinking heavily, becoming more and more drunk. They started sliding their empty beer glasses across the table and smashing them into ours.

"As soon as this started, you could see the look in Nick's eyes – he'd lost it completely - and all of a sudden I thought, 'Oh, no, he's going to blow.' But it seemed his newfound Christianity was holding him back. And he just said to one of the guys, 'Don't do that again. Please don't do that again.'

"So these guys thought that was great and the next guy finishes his glass and slides it across and smashes a glass right next to Nick on the table. Nick jumps out of his seat, grabs the guy, hurls him against the wall and says, 'Listen mate, I'm a Christian first, but I'm getting very angry. If you do that again, I'll kill you.'

"The guy just got back into his chair like he was scared stiff and we didn't hear a word from them for the rest of the evening."

Life as a Christian hasn't always been easy. "Unfortunately during my ten years with the Wallabies, I began to backslide. I read the Bible and prayed only when I needed to, especially before games. My wife, my mother-in-law and I used to pray together before each game. In retrospect, I realise how important it is to be in constant contact with the Lord, to be consistently reading his word and seeking his will for your life. If you have a personal relationship with Jesus, you live a righteous life, and you're constantly seeking his will for your life, then you can't go wrong.

"Sometimes on tour I did things that probably aren't seen as Christian," Nick admits. "I don't want people running around thinking, 'Oh, Nick Farr-Jones is a good Christian.' I want them to hear that I'm not quite the committed person they think I am."

Nick describes his Christian life as "a bit of a roller coaster. It hasn't been solid commitment - throwing the cross over the shoulder each day. For about four years I was solidly committed, but then for whatever reason I stopped getting up early in the morning to read the bible and I didn't do a lot of praying. But since moving to Paris I've been back into it and I realise it's the most important thing in my life."

Nick spent four years in Paris, where we worked in commodities marketing with the Societe Generale bank. Now back in Sydney, he is enjoying life beyond rugby with his family. "I hope I don't lie back on my deathbed and think, 'Nick, there are things which you should have done which you didn't do,' and a lot of these are Christian things - I want the Lord to use me. I know the Lord has plans for me, I'm excited about them. I'm just trying to work out exactly what they are. I hope I get to the end of my life and say, 'I sought the will of God and tried to do that in my life.'"

A.C. GREEN

IRON MAN

A.C. Green is the National Basketball Association's (NBA) undisputed all-time Iron Man. Since running on to the court with the Los Angeles Lakers in 1985, until playing his last game with the Miami Heat in 2001, Green missed just three games – his last on November 18, 1986.

Green's unwavering perseverance and determination were an example and inspiration throughout his streak of 1,192 consecutive games – a streak that continued despite many hurdles. "I've had teeth knocked out," he says. "I've had muscle cramps, a sprained ankle, deep bruises, a broken thumb…"

On November 26, 1999, Green become professional basketball's all-time Iron Man, playing his 1042nd consecutive game against the New Jersey Nets to break Ron Boone's record. Boone played 662 consecutive games in the American Basketball Association (ABA) and 379 in the NBA, from 1968 to 1981.

Fans long suspected Green would become the all-time Iron Man, watching milestones pass along the way. On November

20, 1997, Green earned the NBA's record with his 907th consecutive game, surpassing Randy Smith's mark set from 1972 to 1983.

Immediately after the opening tip-off, the game was halted for a brief ceremony, with a complete acknowledgement of the feat commemorated at half time. Green was presented the game ball, a one-of-a-kind "A.C. Green Iron Man" leather jacket, and a Baltimore Orioles jersey from baseball's Iron Man, Cal Ripkin Jr, who said, "He's a man of character, but also a man with extreme heart."

The forward was finally in the spotlight, recognised for his contributions to his teams and the game as a whole. Sports writer, Alon Marcovici, wrote on the night of the accomplishment, "Green received more attention leading up to today than perhaps in all of his 907 games combined. But it's well-deserved."

"It's been a long time coming," A.C. added. "It means a great deal, I hope everyone can somehow, some way, feel a part of these years of hard work and dedication to my job. It feels great. It's an awesome feeling, but that's a poor choice of words. It's an understatement. I know it's part of my destiny being fulfilled. I don't pursue records, I just love playing the game."

Throughout his career Green was careful not to let his profile affect his character. "From high school to college to the pros, I never perceived myself as a star at any level in athletic competition," he says. "The beginning of the end as an athlete at this level is when you perceive yourself as greater than you are. My mother always told me to remember where I came from."

Green also deflects the credit for his record streak. "God played a big part in my run of consecutive games. There were a lot of days out there I don't know how I made it. You go through some bad spells and sometimes you can do all the preparations - stretching, weight lifting, seeing doctors and taking medicine - but that just doesn't seem like it's enough. Despite this I never allowed myself to take a day off or succumb to what my body told me."

Green explains his longevity as having been sixty-percent spirit, thirty-percent mind, and ten-percent body. The day of his 907th game was spent with his parents at church. "God plays an important part in my life," says the veteran. "I think it's nothing short of the hand of God that has been over my life and that ushered the streak on course. My faith not only helped me try to be the best person off the court, but also to have the goal to please Jesus Christ on the court - with the way I played or the way I prepared myself for the game."

A.C. – whose initials don't stand for anything - also credits the coaches who let him play. The forward's career started with the Lakers, coached by Pat Riley, under whom he sat out his last game. After that, the games-played streak stretched through the Lakers' back-to-back championships in 1987 and 1988, where Green became known as the "Enforcer." He was also named to the Western Conference All-Star team as a starter in 1990.

In September 1993, Green joined the Phoenix Suns as a free agent, garnering his career's best statistics, averaging 14.7 points per game and 9.2 rebounds. Two season's later he played one of his finest games, scoring twenty-nine points and pulling down twenty rebounds against the Clippers on January 9. That season he also broke the 10,000 point barrier against the Toronto Raptors, becoming one of only ten active players to reach 10,000 points and 7,000 rebounds.

During the following season, Green was traded to the Dallas Mavericks where his consistent contributions kept his consecutive games streak extending. With the team he brought up his 1000th straight game in a victory over Vancouver on March 13, 1999. After the game Dallas coach Don Nelson said, "A thousand games in our league is like going to the moon and back."

That year A.C. was traded back to the where his career began in 1985. The move to Los Angeles was just at the right time, the Lakers returning to the glory days when Green was last with the club. On the back of Shaquille O'Neal, the team surged through the 1999-2000 season and playoffs, taking the championship finals against the Indiana Pacers 116-111 in Game 6. The win was Green's third of his career, all of them with the Lakers.

"It's a real blessing," the excited champion said after the game. "I have some great teammates. This whole year has been a lot of fun. It's just a wonderful feeling. It's the result of a whole year of work. It's why you play this game, to get a hold of this trophy.

It's a great thing. I thank God for it. I thank my teammates and the coaching staff. It's a real special group of guys."

To be a champion, Green believes intensity is important. He never succumbed to thoughts he could sit out because he wasn't needed or because his body was telling him to. There were plenty of excuses he could have used to miss a game, but his plan was always to go out and contribute. This was so even during a year with the Lakers when he was kneed continuously in his thighs during practice, to the point of wearing thigh pads for protection to the deep bruises. Or through the 1995-1996 season when he wore a protective face mask for twelve games after an elbow from a New York Knicks player knocked out one of his bottom front teeth and loosened another, which he later pulled out himself in the locker room. Or the time he got a crick in his neck that lasted until the tip-off, recovering just in time. Or through the most difficult injury he has ever had to play with: lower back spasms.

The two metre tall forward is by nature low-key. He may have been aggressive on the court, but his desire is to be a man of integrity. Green was determined to live a godly lifestyle on and off the hardwood.

One of his Phoenix Suns' teammates, Kevin Johnson, remembers when Green was elbowed in the face. "Just take his reaction when that happened," he says. "A.C. just looked at the guy, picked up his tooth and walked out. Nobody in his right mind would react in such a calm manner."

A.C.'s character stems from his Christian upbringing. "I was very religious when growing up in Portland, Oregon," As a high school All-American player, he went to church and made good grades too. But as he headed to Oregon State University, he began to realise being good just to please people wasn't adequate.

"I had a lot of things going for me," says Green. "I was popular, but very empty inside. My church attendance was consistent, but was doing nothing for me personally. I didn't have a relationship with Jesus Christ. I began to see that going to heaven had nothing to do with being good. I had been deceived in this like so many others." On August 2, 1981 Green went to church with his friends and heard the minister ask, "Do you want to go to heaven?" It was the question on his mind.

"As the minister explained that Christ was the way to heaven - that he came to die on the cross for the sins of everyone and was raised from the dead to provide eternal life for all who believed - I knew I had to make a decision. It was definitely a crossroad in my life.

"Did I want to be committed to Jesus - to not be one who seeks to please people, but please God? There were 150 people in the church, but that day God targeted me and I was born again - as John 3:3 says every person should be. That's the most exciting thing that has happened in my life so far. I'm a Christian who loves God and just tries to live by his principles daily."

A.C. was particularly inspiried by Jesus' command to seek first God's kingdom and his righteousness, as recorded in Matthew

6:33. "I want to put God first in everything," Green says. "That was the very first thing I learnt when I became a Christian – don't let the gospel become second to anything, don't let peer pressure place it in second or third position, don't let friendships place it in second or third position, don't let family place it in second or third position, but seek first the kingdom of God and all of its righteousness, and all other things will be taken care of."

Green's conversion indirectly earned him a lot of media coverage over the years. While in college he drew attention not only for his playing abilities but also for protesting the sale of Playboy at the campus bookstore, even though the magazine was heralding him as an All-American. After this incident, as A.C. would take free throws during a game, opposition supporters would hold up centrefolds behind the backboard.

When not on the court, Green spent his time involved in Christian and community work. He has served as a director for Challenge for Christ, an organisation dedicated to train, build and develop professional and college athletes. "We want to help them gain a sense of substance, not just talk. They must know what they are talking about and know how to minister to others," he says. "I want to see athletes who won't be egotistical, but submissive to Jesus. That's where the real power comes from."

The A.C. Green Youth Foundation oversees a number of projects, such as an after-school program with a built-in obligation that parents become involved. Building a strong family structure incorporating family values and bonding is important to Green.

Green's foundation presents a positive alternative to the notorious sexual exploits of NBA players. Athletes for Abstinence brought together well-known athletes from the National Football League and the NBA to produce a video, It Ain't Worth It, with teens and medical experts to get across the message that sexual abstinence is possible and preferable.

The foundation also sponsors a free basketball camp that develops young basketballers' skills. In the afternoons, the kids are taken on field trips to different companies to increase their awareness of the job market. Again, the family is included in the award ceremony to build up the family structure.

With Green's days on the court over, he now focuses on his youth and community work and has also been appointed as Vice President of Basketball Operations with the ABA's Southern California Surf. "Having a person with A.C.'s basketball knowledge and respect throughout the basketball world is just termendous," Surf owner and president Steve Chase said. "More important than his basketball reputation, A.C.'s personal reputation, moral character and charitable involvements are second to none. He is a fantastic role model who promotes a positive message to our youth."

Over sixteen seasons, A.C. claimed three championship rings and set an Iron Man record many believe will never be broken. In his 1,278 games, he scored 12,331 points and pulled down 9,473 rebounds. "My goal was to play every game," Green says. "Winning the championship was a goal. But I admit my streak is right up there with the championship years."

Green has another goal he wishes to continue fulfilling. "Through my relationship with God," he says, "and time spent with other Christians, I have experienced what it is to have quality, meaningful relationships. And I have come to better appreciate the importance of being a good role model for others. It is my hope that some may come to know Christ as they see me live for him."

This chapter was written with the help of Jennie Chandler

PENNY HEYNS

MAKING WAVES

In 1999, Penny Heyns became regarded as swimming's golden girl. At the Janet Evans Invitational meet in July, she broke a world record each of the four times she dived into the pool, first in the 200m breaststroke heat and final, and then in the 100m heat and final.

"Every time I swim like that, it blows me away," Heyns said after becoming the first swimmer to hold all three breaststroke distance records simultaneously. "It's like I'm blessed. Coming into this meet, I was feeling tired. Never in my dreams did I think this would happen. If I thought of them as world record swims, I'd really be too overwhelmed." Her achievement is even more amazing considering she was in midseason training, unshaven and unrested.

Penny's remarkable form continued into the Pan Pacific Championships in Sydney a few weeks later. In her first race of the meet Heyns again lowered her 100m breaststroke world record mark. This feat of setting five world records in five consecutive starts is itself believed to be a world record for all sports.

Penny continued through the week picking up gold medals in the 100m and 200m, and setting two world records in the 200m and one in the 50m in a special time trial. The world governing body for swimming, FINA, has rated Heyns' swim in the 50m, with a time of 30.83s, as the best swimming performance ever, across all disciplines, as at September 2, 1999.

One year later at the Sydney Olympics, Heyns was expected to repeat her golden double from Atlanta, but things didn't go to plan. In the 100m final, the South African led from the front but a late charge from sixteen-year-old American Megan Quann and fifteen-year-old Australian Leisel Jones saw her relegated to Bronze.

Two days later Heyns' Olympic campaign, and her career, came to an end when she was eliminated in the heats of the 200m. "I didn't expect to go further," she said after the race. "I wanted to go out there and enjoy myself. So often we focus on the gold medal or the world record and we miss out on so much, so I really wanted to experience it all. I know I've struggled this season. I didn't have the legs."

The South African has always been well regarded by fellow competitors. Australian rival, Samantha Riley said at the Pan Pacs, "I think Penny is a great swimmer. I've been competing against her since the 1992 Olympics and it has always been a friendly rivalry. She's a nice person out of the pool and great to chat to. I enjoy racing her a lot and she is one of the best breaststrokers in the world."

Canadian swimmer, Joanne Malar, who trained with Penny in Calgary, added: "It's really motivating training and swimming with her. I remember in 1996 watching her swim and saying hello to her, but I didn't really know her. Then she moved to Calgary the week before me. She's such a friendly person. The cool thing about her is that she helps me swim breaststroke as well. She's not one of these people where there is tension between two rivals. When Penny sees me do a good breaststroke set, she'll tell me. It's nice to have a friend like that who is a friend in and out of the pool. It's really motivating swimming with someone who is a double Olympic gold medallist and who is down-to-earth like other people I know."

Penny has come a long way since she was head girl at Amanzimtoti High School on the Natal south coast. She started swimming at seven and by sixteen had already won gold in the 100m and 200m breaststroke at the Senior Nationals, and held the South African record in the 100m. The medals kept coming, her list of achievements seemingly endless.

"To be a world class swimmer," Penny says, "takes quite a bit of talent, but talent without a lot of hard work, dedication and the right opportunities is not enough. I have been blessed with a lot of natural ability where swimming, particularly breaststroke, is concerned, but I believe it is by God's grace I was given the right opportunities to develop that talent." Penny's family has also been a constant source of encouragement to her, even though she has spent many years far away from them while training in North America.

In 1992, Heyns was chosen as the youngest member of the South African Olympic team for Barcelona. She finished thirty-third in the 100m breaststroke and thirty-fourth in the 200m. Nebraska State University soon offered her a scholarship which she took up in January 1993. In September of the same year, she was placed under a new coach, Jan Bidrman.

It was this successful partnership which took her to the 1994 Commonwealth Games (bronze in the 100m), the 1994 World Championships (sixth in the 100m, thirteenth in the 200m), the 1995 Pan Pacific Games (first in the 100m, second in the 200m), the 1995 World Student Games (first place and new world games records in the 100m and 200m) and the 1995 All Africa Games (first in the 100m and 200m).

Not surprisingly, Heyns was ranked first in the world for the 100m and 200m breaststroke in 1995. Her success continued into 1996, setting a new world record in the 100m at the South African Olympic Trials.

The 1996 Atlanta Olympics are the highlight of Heyns' swimming career. Not only did she win gold in both the 100m and 200m breaststroke, the first time in history that anyone had won the double, she also set new world and Olympic records in the 100m (1:07.02 in a preliminary race) and a new Olympic record in the 200m (2:25.41).

"The two races were very different," Penny says. "Since I already owned the hundred, I expected to break my own record again and thus stood a good chance of winning. I set out in the heats of the hundred to break the record. I did however expect to go a little faster than I went and that others might also go better. Luckily for me no one else did and that left me swimming more than a second faster than the next person.

"I guess I felt more a sense of relief when I won the hundred. I knew I could do it if it was God's will, and that the whole country was watching and expecting. The two hundred was a bit of a surprise. I am not usually a great two hundred swimmer, but knew I stood a chance if I swam my best time. I had to get out fast and hope no one would catch me. It was a great feeling to have won the two hundred, and a bonus to find out no one had ever won both in the same Olympics before.

"It was all the Lord though. The last fifty of that two hundred was so hard, but the Lord carried me all the way to the finish and now all the glory must go to him. The most special thing about my whole experience was knowing I couldn't have done it without the Lord, and thus that he had a greater plan for my life of which swimming was just a tiny detail. I can't wait to see what's next."

Penny says winning in the Olympics is a dream for many people. Her dream came true in 1996, but the fulfillment she found in her achievements was not lasting. "After I won there was a great feeling of satisfaction, but that didn't last long. At that time I realised how important winning had become to me, and that even though I still prayed and read my Bible, I wasn't walking as closely to the Lord as I needed to. I still felt this little space in my heart that was unsatisfied and empty. I had drifted from the intimacy I once shared with the Lord when I was young, and now I missed it.

"All the commotion after my wins was fun but left me longing for that closeness even more, especially since everyone was now my buddy and I no longer knew what was real or who I really was. I tried to please everyone while just getting myself more and more into a knot and unsure what the purpose behind everything was. I felt a tremendous responsibility to do something with the platform I now had, and knew God had allowed it all to happen for a reason. The pressure was on stronger than ever.

"Jan also moved away and this left me to swim on my own. I also wasn't sure if I still wanted to continue swimming and why I was doing it. Suddenly all these new, external reasons sprung up.

"I was unhappy and was swimming progressively worse as the 1997 season went on. Around April I finally woke up and rededicated my life to the Lord Jesus. One day I read Jeremiah 29:11-13. The Holy Spirit spoke to me when I read: 'If you seek me you will find me when you seek me with all your heart.' I decided I would seek the Lord with all my heart in every way I could. Nothing is more important to me.

"I believe those bad swims were needed so I would come to the end of myself and my reasons and ambitions in swimming."

To Heyns, being a Christian and having a relationship with God means everything. "I've realised being a Christian is so much more than just going to church, reading your Bible everyday and saying a short prayer before continuing with your day as you please. It means having an intimate relationship with Jesus and letting him be in control of your life. Living intimately with the Lord has been an exciting journey that brings more joy and fulfillment than any other achievement I've ever been blessed with, and the most exciting moment is yet to come on the day I meet my lord face-to-face. The journey is not over yet and I believe it will never be.

"It has become so clear to me that this world is temporary and thus the reality of an eternity with Christ so exciting. I believe however, that the Kingdom of Christ is within as we live for him. No gold medal or world record ever gave me the peace and sense of wholeness I have found in having an intimate relationship with the creator of the universe. Nothing is more exciting and meaningful than knowing the love of Christ and knowing one day I will wake up to see him face-to-face for eternity. What prize can be greater than that?"

Despite a hectic schedule, Penny takes time to read the Bible, drawing her strength from God's word. "I always try to begin my day with a quiet time. If I lay my day before the Lord from the start, then things will go according to his will. It is important that we as believers invite the Holy Spirit to take control of our lives from the moment we wake up. The word says we are 'more than conquerors through Him who loved us (Romans 8: 37).' Depending on the Lord at all times and always knowing he always works all things for the good of those who love him and who are called by his name, gives me the strength to endure and live a victorious life in Christ."

Heyns knows her swimming talent was a gift from God and now she wants to use the benefits of those talents to glorify him, even though it isn't easy. She has the assurance that one day she will receive a reward in heaven is far greater than any gold medal, but she also knows true fulfillment here on earth comes from a heart that is right with God.

"Without God," she says, "my life would be empty and without meaning. He gives me a purpose and a hope. Achievements are temporary and shallow if they are not given over to the Lord so he can do what he wills with them. My life would be incomplete without Jesus."

This chapter was written with the help of Gillian Turner

BRIAN IRVINE

LIVING DETERMINATION

In mid-1995, Scottish international footballer Brian Irvine went to his family doctor worried about a persistent sensation in his foot. The defender was a little surprised when the doctor referred him to the local hospital.

"I was feeling pleased, in total ignorance, thinking this would clear up the problem and it would be all right," Irvine remembers in his autobiography, *What a Difference a Day Makes*. "After the weekend passed, the doctor came into my side ward on the Monday and started explaining how he felt that in time these sensations should settle down and hopefully everything would be back to normal. Although he had never treated a professional sportsman, I should be able to continue as before.

"At this point I was a bit suspicious as to why he should mention my career and that things should be okay. But worse was to follow. 'I cannot say how long it will take to clear,' he said. 'It is likely to clear, but how long I don't know.'

"I remember thinking that it was only five or six weeks until pre-season, and hoped it would clear up by then. Then the doctor mentioned one or two other points, and with these thoughts in my head I was distracted from his general line of talk until I heard the words 'multiple sclerosis' mentioned.

"He spoke on, of what I've no idea, then left the room, closed the door. I was sitting on the bed alone when it suddenly hit me. My pulse raced. I felt hot. I felt claustrophobic. I thought I was going to be physically sick. My eyes were full of tears. I prayed, not long, not clever prayers, but I prayed to the Lord to be close, to be my strength.

"It was like someone saying, 'You're dying but it is not as bad as it sounds.' I understood the seriousness of multiple sclerosis but I couldn't relate my symptoms to something that could finish my career."

Brian's career was one that might never have started. He was always a useful footballer, yet at nineteen when most footballers had already been on professional contracts for two years and were breaking into the first team, Brian found himself working as a bank clerk and playing semi-professional football for Falkirk. His boyhood dreams of playing for his beloved Aberdeen and even Scotland seemed destined to be no more than that.

In the 1983-84 season he played his first game in the Falkirk first team. The following season he was a regular. His performances on the field attracted interest from English league sides Nottingham Forest and Charlton Athletic, but when an offer came from Aberdeen manager, Alex Ferguson, the decision was simple. His dream move came true, becoming the last player Alex Ferguson signed before moving to Manchester United.

Rangers and Celtic now dominate Scottish football, but in the mid-80s Aberdeen had that honour. The club won the League two years in a row, in 1983-84 and 1984-85, and the Scottish Cup three years running from 1982-84. They also claimed the European Cup Winners' Cup in 1983 and reached the semi-final the following season.

Irvine had a successful career at Aberdeen, playing with the club as they won the Scottish Cup in 1990, and the League Cup in 1989 and 1995. In addition there were three losing finals, several semi-finals and five second-place finishes in the League.

The 1992-93 season summed up the frustration of being Scotland's second best team. Aberdeen finished second to Rangers in the League, and lost both cup finals to the team by a single goal.

As expected, Brian was a reserve, playing just one league game in his first season. He played twenty in his second, then seventeen, then twenty-seven. In the following season, 1989-90, he was an established first choice player.

Aberdeen reached the Scottish Cup final in 1990. Defence dominated the game, the scoreboard reading nil-all after ninety minutes, and the same after extra time. For the first time the destiny of the Scottish Cup was to be settled in a penalty shoot-out. Each team nominated five penalty-takers. The result: four-all. Now it was sudden death with teams taking penalties in turn, the first team ahead after an equal number of shots would be the winner.

The defender's main aim at this stage was to get to the back of the queue. The strikes continued, Celtic leading eight-seven, Aberdeen needing the equaliser. "It was a measure of my self-confidence as a penalty taker that I was more than happy to let seventeen-year-old Graeme Watson take the ninth penalty," Brian remembers. "He scores. It's eight-all.

"Celtic's Anton Rogan hits a good penalty towards the bottom left corner. Our keeper Theo Snelders takes off, gets his fingertips to the ball and pushes it around the post. It's still eight-all.

"There is nowhere to hide. I am down for the next penalty. There were only two Aberdeen players who had not taken penalties, Snelders and me.

"I was really nervous as I stepped up to take the kick. I just said a prayer and put my faith in God. The moment the ball hit the net was fantastic. It's a feeling I will never be able to describe. If I took another penalty tomorrow I would probably miss. I can't take penalties. I wasn't very confident.

"I decided to hit it to the goalkeeper's left. As I stepped up, I saw Pat Bonner gamble and move early to his right. For a split second I knew if I hit it properly I would score. The penalty shoot-out was at the Aberdeen end, and as the ball went in the Aberdeen supporters erupted in a sea of red."

Four months later Brian's career moved up a level. After the Scottish side for a European Championship game against Romania was depleted by injuries, Brian arrived home from church to a ringing telephone. Manager Andy Roxburgh wanted him to join the team immediately. Brian played in the game and made a total of nine full international appearances for Scotland.

Irvine had fulfilled his two main childhood dreams, playing for Aberdeen and Scotland, but it was not his success on the field that gave him the strength to face MS, that came from his Christian faith.

Brian's faith had its origins in his teens. He had a Christian background and went to church regularly, but it didn't mean much to him. One day talking with some teammates challenged his thinking.

"On the way to football at Falkirk," the defender remembers, "we started talking about the purpose of life. Someone mentioned that the Bible said Jesus was coming back. Neither of my teammates in the car were Christians, but we had a good discussion about religion, the world and the problems of the day.

"After that game I went home and was alone. I couldn't get what was said out of my mind. I opened up the Bible and read from the gospels. What I had read before at Sunday school and church suddenly changed and became real. I realised God loved me and had demonstrated it in such a wonderful way, by Jesus dying for me on the cross. That was the turning point. That was the night I became a Christian."

In the months after his MS diagnosis, Brian was tested to the limit. He worked in an industry prone to seeing a defensive error as a "disaster", and the outcome of a "vital" game as a matter of "life and death". However, as Brian contemplated the end of his career, life in a wheelchair and even death, Aberdeen's results didn't seem so important.

There were many dark days. Shortly after discharge from hospital, he went on a family holiday. There were some wonderful times but also "nights whilst the family was asleep when I would slip upstairs in the lodge and cry my eyes dry and pray to my Lord as never before." Another time Brian went off and spent a few days in a hotel on his own, without telling anyone where he was. He felt he needed to be on his own to think. Brian now recognises his foolishness. Not telling anyone where he was going caused a great deal anxiety for his wife, Donna, and his close friends.

One aspect of this period, which seems amusing in retrospect but was less so at the time, was the letters he received. One read, "Dear Brian, I am sorry to hear you have MS. My brother had MS and he died last year…" It didn't exactly encourage.

Some words were a great source of strength however, and these came from the Bible. Romans 8:28 says, "And we know that in all things God works for the good of those who love him, who have been called according to his purpose."

Psalm 23 was also a comfort: "The Lord is my shepherd, I shall not be in want… Even though I walk through the valley of the shadow of death, I will fear no evil, for you are with me; your rod and your staff, they comfort me. You prepare a table before me in the presence of my enemies. You anoint my head with oil; my cup overflows. Surely goodness and love will follow me all the days of my life, and I will dwell in the house of the Lord forever."

At the time of his MS diagnosis, Aberdeen was due to start pre-season training. Brian started his comeback at this point too. While the rest of the players ran endlessly, Brian would walk two miles and was more exhausted than they were.

His walk took an hour, then he managed it in fifty-five minutes, then fifty. He began jogging the last bit, and then a bit more, until eventually he was jogging the whole way. The next stage was gym work and eventually full training.

By mid October, Brian had enough training behind him to get on the park. Aberdeen had a friendly away against Ross County, and he was named as a sub. "It was like getting ready to play in a cup-final but without any of the hype. I was kicking a ball again and it felt funny. I was trying to judge heading a ball coming through the air and regain the skills I had not used for months." He played forty-five minutes and slotted a goal. He was back.

His first touch in a competitive game could hardly have been more traumatic, coming on as a sub against Kilmarnock. "After I had been on the field for two minutes, the ball broke to me and I laid it to Dean Windass in midfield, and then I blacked out. For a split second I wondered what was happening to me, then realised that it wasn't me but that the floodlights had failed."

Brian continued to make progress and not only regained his place in the Aberdeen team but even fulfilled a remaining professional ambition by captaining. Irvine stayed with the club until May 1997, tallying 308 league appearances and twenty-eight goals in his twelve years.

The defender signed with Dundee, staying for two years before moving to Ross County in June 1999. Despite being a former international who scored the winning goal in a Scottish Cup Final, Irvine feels no bitterness at playing out his twilight years at a lower division club. On the contrary, he considers himself fortunate to be able to still make a living playing the game he loves.

"Being offered a three-year deal so late in my career was very important," he says. "Also I had played at the top level all my career and I liked the idea of giving something back to the game and helping younger players."

Irvine was also impressed by how well run, ambitious and forward-looking the club was. Under the leadership of Neale Cooper, the side gained promotion from Third to First Division in successive seasons from 1998/99.

Playing with Ross County, the footballer aims to express his faith on the field, as he has tried throughout his career. Despite trying, Irvine admits he has not always got it right.

"At times, particularly earlier in my career," he says, "I have been prone to bring things home. If I have had a bad game I wasn't great company for Donna and the children. I have had to ask God to help me keep things in perspective."

Playing defence, Brian's first job is to win his one-to-one battle with the forward he is marking. In these intimate encounters, verbal abuse is common as players seek a psychological advantage. "It is part of the game and it is best to ignore it and not let it get to me. On occasions, I am sorry to say, I have let it rile me and found myself exchanging insults with my opponent. I need the Lord's help in these situations.

"I remember a game I played in for Aberdeen against Rangers. I committed a foul. The player I fouled got up and pushed me to the ground. I got up quickly and went to confront him and then was able just to walk away. I am sure it was the grace of God, as my human instinct was to retaliate. I don't always get it right but in these situations I seek to express my Christian faith on the pitch."

Irvine hoped to complete his career without being sent off, but has twice been shown the red card. One was for Dundee against Motherwell for two yellow cards. "The first yellow card was for a hand-ball and the other for a clumsy high tackle. Another referee on another day might not have given a yellow card for either incident. I remember sitting in the dressing room afterwards thinking, 'I've blown it. I've let everyone down. I have let the team down and I have let down the standard of Christian witness I try to express in my football career.' I felt harshly treated but at the end of the day what I thought didn't matter as the official had sent me off."

Playing for Ross County against Ayr United in 2000, Brian earned his second red card. As an Ayr player made a run on goal Brian made a tackle. He felt he had got the ball, but the referee deemed he had taken the man and awarded a penalty. Moreover he decided that Brian had been the last defender and therefore denied a goal-scoring opportunity and sent him off. "I was very down about it at the time. I was club captain and I felt I had let the team down. To make matters worse, Ayr scored the penalty and we lost 1-0."

Reflecting on the two sendings-off, Brian is still disappointed they happened. "I wish I could have gone through my career without being sent off but it was not to be. This illustrates the tightrope I walk every time I step on the park as a Christian professional footballer. Take the Ross County incident, I had to make the tackle. I thought I could get the ball. I think I did get the ball. But I was sent off and in some people's eyes, blew my witness. But would it have been a better or worse witness if I had not tried to make the tackle?

"One thing I always try to ask myself is, 'What was my intent?' On that occasion my intent was to make a fair tackle. Committing a professional foul and bringing the player down was never in my mind. On other occasions I have to admit I have made reckless tackles - when someone has wound me up. These are ones I have to acknowledge as wrong and seek the Lord's forgiveness for."

Brian has left a lasting impression on those he has dealt with throughout his career. Craig Brown, the Scotland manager for most of Irvine's international appearances, sums up: "We are dealing here with an outstanding gentleman who just happens to be a professional footballer. I am sure that, in any walk of life, Brian Irvine would be a credit to his profession and, of course, to his beloved family. No praise is high enough for a guy who is one of the finest people I have come across in my thirty-eight years in professional football."

This chapter was written by Stuart Weir

MICHAEL JONES

ICEMAN

In 1986, Michael Jones began a rugby career remembered for its moments of brilliance, serious injuries and his uncompromising Christian stand. Beginning as a representative of Western Samoa, his country of birth, and continuing with the New Zealand All Blacks, Michael became one of rugby's best forwards.

Former Australian player, David Campese said: "Michael is one of the greatest players in world rugby because he is extremely skilful, a great athlete and a great guy. He knows the game inside and out and he's a great team player. He's very strong and obviously very smart. He always plays to the best of his ability and never gives a bad performance. He's always a nightmare for the Wallabies."

Michael's talent was first recognised in 1977 when, as a twelve-year-old, he stood out at a primary and intermediate schoolboys rugby tournament. Five years later, he captained Henderson High School's First XV to a 394-point season victory, with only thirty-nine points conceded. In those days, Henderson High School was scoffed at for its rather loose and liberal approach to education. As a First XV side, they should have posed little threat to other contenders, but instead convincingly beat everyone they played and wound up winning the Auckland secondary schools B-grade championship.

Not surprisingly, a number of onlookers were shocked by the outcome and interested in the young man who helped it happen. Within days, and barely out of school, Michael was invited to attend senior practice at local club Waitemata and soon played Auckland club rugby.

In 1985, after Canterbury lost the Ranfurly Shield to Auckland in New Zealand's National Provincial Competition (NPC), Michael's first major break came. He played for the under twenty-one-year-olds in the curtain raiser and caught the eye of Auckland coach John Hart. Hart had previously decided if Auckland would win the shield, he would recruit two of the Colts for the remainder of their southern tour. He chose Michael and Bernie McCahill. Several days later in his first game for Auckland, Michael scored three tries against South Canterbury.

Rugby columnist Spiro Zavos recalls how he later saw Michael's tries on video. "Here was the complete player," he wrote. "He seemed able to totally and instinctively understand the dynamics of the game." Soon everybody was talking about the future of young Michael Jones.

Michael's international debut was in 1986 for Western Samoa against Wales. His performance in this match was so impressive the New Zealand selectors convinced the twenty-two-year-old, who had lived in Auckland since childhood, to play for the All Blacks in the inaugural Rugby World Cup in 1987.

Michael had a sensational tournament, scoring the first try for the All Blacks in both their first and final games against Italy and France. He was regarded as player of the tournament and hailed as a hero by the New Zealand public.

"Winning the first World Cup back in 1987 was special for a number of reasons," the forward says. "That was the first World Cup, we were playing here in New Zealand, and we had a team that was playing very good rugby. We totally dominated the tournament. It was my first year in the All Blacks too, so that World Cup victory will always be a special occasion for me."

At the World Cup, Michael set a standard of play he continued throughout his career. Former New Zealand captain, John Graham, said of him: "He's naturally gifted at running the right lines, has amazingly good reflexes and is very fast over thirty metres. His hand, eye and foot coordination is remarkable. He has a natural instinct for loose forward play. It's God-given. On the paddock, there's a dominating presence, a magnetic pattern to his football. He's so often in the middle of what's going on."

Along the way, Michael has experienced several career-threatening injuries. In 1989, he injured his right knee while playing against Argentina and was forced out of the game for a year. Eight years later, playing in the first Test of the year against Fiji, Jones sustained a serious injury to his left knee.

After the game the *Sydney Morning Herald* wrote: "Another serious knee injury to incomparable flanker Michael Jones has taken some gloss off the All Blacks' 71-5 win over Fiji in their first Test of the year at Albany. Jones went down heavily in a tackle in the thirty-eighth minute of Saturday night's game and later required surgery on a ruptured patella tendon in his left knee... All Blacks doctor John Mayhew said Jones, 32, would be out of all rugby for the rest of the year, which throws doubt on whether the blind-side flanker, one of the game's greatest players, will wear an All Black jersey again. He has won fifty-one Test caps in a superb career, badly affected by injury, and scored his thirteenth Test try against Fiji on Saturday night."

Michael experienced some tough times, but believes his faith in Jesus Christ has given him the strength to keep going. The foundations of Michael's faith were laid when he was a child. Born in 1965, he was raised with his brother and two sisters in West Auckland. His childhood was fairly happy despite the death of his father when he was four-years-old. His mother, Maina Wearne-Jones, kept the family close by embracing them together in regular prayer times and family fellowship. As a result, Michael heard about the Christian faith at a very young age and was quick to respond.

"I actually asked the Lord into my life when I was seven-years-old," he says, "and I believe from that day on I knew God was a very big part of my life. Growing up, however, you go through stages where you take things for granted. Being brought up in a Christian home I started to cruise a bit. A real turning point for me was when I injured my knee playing for New Zealand. Although I was a Christian at that point in my life, I really had to reassess where I was with my relationship with Christ. Through that whole incident, that whole experience, I started to sort things out and become a lot more serious with my faith. It is still a learning process and I'm still growing in the Lord, but I'm thankful the Lord has always been faithful to me. I'm continuing to grow in the Lord, it's a constant walk, it's a daily process."

At seven, Michael didn't know it, but his relationship with God would one day become a controversial issue throughout rugby circles. When the All Black announced he was not going to play on Sundays, his decision became a highly publicised and debated issue - one with serious repercussions, causing him to be the subject of public and media scrutiny, as well as costing him some major matches, including all of the 1995 Rugby World Cup.

"Many people ask me why I don't play on Sundays," Jones says. "It's a personal thing between me and God. As a family, we always learnt to honour the Lord and especially set one day aside to spend with him and our loved ones, not seeking after our own pleasures."

Michael also believes if people have taken notice of God as a result, then it has all been worth it. "If my decision not to play on Sundays has made people more aware of the reality of God, that's more than I've been able to achieve physically on the rugby field."

Rugby is an important aspect of his life, but it pales in significance to knowing and doing God's will. "Although I am truly honoured to represent New Zealand on the rugby field, my first allegiance is definitely to my lord and saviour, Jesus Christ. People easily forget a player after he stops playing, but one thing I'd like to be remembered for is that I was a person who put God first before rugby."

Michael also believes as a Christian, God sustains him through difficult times. The infamous knee injury in 1989 at Athletic Park, which was heard twenty metres away, should have ended his career, but Michael spent the ensuing months seeking direction from God and being inspired by passages from the Bible, such as Isaiah 40: "Even youths grow tired and weary, and young men stumble and fall; but those who hope in the Lord will renew their strength. They will soar on wings like eagles; they will run and not grow weary, they will walk and not be faint." Even though Michael knew this passage didn't necessarily mean he would play rugby again, he did know he would be given all the strength he needed to achieve God's purpose for him, whatever that may be.

Since Michael's injury against Fiji in 1997, life has been anything but kind to him. In November that year, the harshest blow was dealt when his mother, Maina Wearne-Jones, died after a four-wheel-drive vehicle she was travelling in crashed and rolled. The news of her death came as a terrible shock to all who knew her, and Michael, her youngest child, was devastated. Since his father's death, Maina had been a pivotal force in his life. "She became my all and I can't express how much I adore her," Michael says.

As a young boy, he remembers how his mother would always tell him if he put God first in his life he couldn't go wrong.

"There is a bigger picture in everything that happens," she would say. These and other pearls of wisdom Maina left behind have been instrumental in guiding Michael through his life. Though she is sadly missed, Michael says he and his family "are immensely comforted by the knowledge we know exactly where she is. This is what she lived for. We are holding on to our memories and the many wonderful things she instilled in our lives."

Only months after the tragedy of his mother's death, Michael had to come to terms with being axed from the All Blacks. Despite working his way back into the side after a year off recovering from injury - one that most people were convinced would see the end of his career - Jones was dropped from the team. Coach John Hart was forced to let him go after a string of consecutive losses called for some urgent reshuffling of the team. Michael seemed the logical choice as his performance and speed had deteriorated since the previous year's injury.

With his days of playing for his country over, Michael decided to play one more season for his provincial side, Auckland. The 1999 season turned out to be a fitting farewell. Auckland made it through to the NPC final, and in his last game, Michael displayed the character for which he will be remembered.

While on the bottom of a ruck, Michael received a cheap shot from one of the Wellington players, opening up a fifteen-centimetre gash on his inner arm. Auckland doctor, Graham Patterson remembers the edges of the cut were six centimetres apart, the muscle had been sliced and the bone was showing. But Michael was determined to play out the last thirty-five minutes of his career. "A lot of people would have called it quits," Patterson says, "but there was no way he wanted that. He kept saying, 'Just get me back out there.'"

After a dozen stitches and more painkiller injections than the doctor can remember, Jones returned to the field, picking himself up from injury as he has done so many times in his career. The loose forward was inspirational for his team, captain Paul Thomson adding, "Suddenly there would be a blue blur and it would be Michael Jones smashing them down."

After the twenty-four to eighteen victory, Jones was carried on the shoulders of his teammates, celebrating a victory lap of his career. "I know I'll miss the guys and the team environment," he said in the change room after the game, "but I'll always keep in contact. I'll always be here for them. Hopefully, they'll see me as their big brother. I've had ups and downs in the game but that is what you learn to live with. Rugby has taught me a lot about life."

Michael's career is over, but as he sees it, God predetermined his days of rugby anyway and they were never dependant on his own ability or will. He is also sure of his relationship with Jesus Christ, and confident that his future is in the hands of a God who "works for the good of those who love him."

This chapter was written with Jannine Pennycook

BERNARD LANGER

CHANGING PRIORITIES

In the Ryder Cup between Europe and the United States in 1991, millions of viewers watched the tournament come down to the last putt on the final hole. Playing on the Ocean Course at Kiawah Island, South Carolina, Bernard Langer had a two-metre putt to keep the Cup in European hands, a miss would give victory to America. The hopes of the European team rested upon Langer's putt.

On the autumn afternoon, the course was overflowing with spectators who looked on silently, anxiously, as Langer paced around the ball and the hole, considering his putt from every conceivable angle. The German addressed the ball, one foot on either side, his body inclined over it. He drew back his putter, then smoothly brought it into contact with the ball, guiding it towards the hole. As the ball veered to the right, Langer lent back in anguish, the American crowd erupting in joy. The United States had won the Ryder Cup, 14.5 to 13.5.

"I was very disappointed," Langer says. "I didn't want to let my teammates down. We played all week very hard to win this Ryder Cup and it all came down to this very last putt from six feet. The main thing was really my concern for them. They really didn't blame me for anything. They tried to make me feel better, but I still felt very disappointed."

Six years later, playing in Europe, the score was again 14.5 to 13.5, but this time in Europe's favour. The Ryder Cup had again come down to rest upon the abilities of Langer, and now he lived up to them and snared victory.

Bernard was born in Anhausen, Germany, in 1957, where his father had settled after escaping from a Russian prisoner of war train en route to Siberia. It was in Anhausen also that Langer first got involved in golf. "My older brother was caddying to earn some pocket money," he says. "We come from a very poor family; we never received any pocket money. When I was about eight-years-old, I asked my brother, Erwin, to take me along to the golf course so I could caddy and earn some money."

After saving for four years, the Bavarian boy bought his first set of clubs. It was clear that he had natural talent and, three years later, he turned professional.

Langer's career has been impeded by a putting condition known as "the yips" but, despite this, he has risen to among the top golfers in the world, winning over fifty tournaments.

Langer's first tournament win came in the Cacharel Under-25s Championship in 1979, when he won by a record seventeen strokes. In the eighties and nineties he cemented himself among the world's best, providing many memorable moments - winning the US Masters in 1985 and 1993, the PGA

Championship in 1995, and the individual title at the 1993 World Cup. Bernard was also integral to the Ryder Cup team in 1993 as the Europeans won for the first time in twenty-eight years. Two years later, he also helped them win on US soil for the first time in sixty years.

Many followers of the game also remember Langer for his shot out of a tree during the 1982 Benson and Hedges tournament, one of the most recognised images of the European tour.

Langer is one of the most respected players on the tour, as former world-number-one Greg Norman testifies: "I've known Bernard since playing the European tour together back in '76. When you grow up with someone on a tour, like we have, you get to know them very well because you get to see their different personalities, you get to see what they're going through in life. One thing about Bernard is that he's always been consistent. That is a real credit to him, because a lot of people change with success, but he hasn't. I admire that in somebody.

"He is also loyal to his word, which is another great thing about him. If he says he's going to be there and do something for you, then he's going to be there and do something for you. They're the kind of things you admire in a guy. I've helped him out a lot over the years and I know he's helped me out a lot."

At the Lakes course in Sydney, Australia, playing in the 1999 Greg Norman Holden International, something happened which reflects the character of this golfer. Needing only par on the last hole to win the tournament, Langer was considering a nine-foot putt when he inadvertently picked up his marker before replacing the ball. No one saw the infringement, but regardless he summoned the rules official onto the green and informed him of what had happened, incurring a one-stroke penalty and losing the tournament. Despite all that had happened, he remained remarkably composed.

"I don't know, I just picked it up," he said. "It's never happened before and it happened today. Don't ask me why I did it. I didn't do it on purpose; it just happened. I was probably too much focused on what I was trying to do."

The significance of Langer's actions was magnified by the two year draught he had experienced since last winning the German Masters in 1997. It would be two more years before he would add another champion's trophy to his cabinet, victory finally coming at the 2001 Dutch Open. There Langer carded an eagle and four birdies on the closing eight holes to force a sudden-death play-off with England's Warren Bennett. The forty-three year-old won the title on the first extra hole, taking the prize for the third time in three different decades.

Langer made sure the wait between wins wasn't as long the next time, seizing the German Masters less than three months later with a score of twenty-two-under. The title was the local's eleventh in his home country and his biggest prize cheque on the European Tour, worth 450,000 euro. Langer's victory also propelled him to third on the European Order of Merit and eleventh in the world rankings.

Bernard Langer is a man of character and he has needed it at many times throughout his career to cope with the yips. They first appeared when Langer was playing on the European tour at eighteen, and have haunted him three times during his career, nearly ending it in 1988.

"It's like a muscle spasm," he explains. "You hold the putter and sometimes you can't take it back. You freeze or you just jerk. Your muscles do something and your hands feel like they're not part of your body. I had times when they wouldn't give me a one foot putt in a match play tournament because they knew the chance I would miss was greater than the chance I would make it. I remember one occasion where I four putted from three feet."

This was a very low point in Bernard's life. "I led one tournament after two rounds, I was ten under, and the next two days I shot five over. From that day on, I had the yips again. They wouldn't go away. I had them for about five or six months. I missed every cut and I went from the very top to the very bottom. I could not see my way out of this. I was a believer by then and I prayed to God: 'Lord, if you want me to do something else, if you don't want me to play golf, tell me where you want me. Tell me what to do, and I'll do it.'"

Langer was ready to bring his professional golfing days to a premature end. "I worked hard to get there and was very fortunate, but when you go through that for five or six months... I know how good I was before and there was nothing left. There wasn't even five percent left. I was ready to give up.

"I was very fortunate that just before I gave up a friend of mine came over and spent a couple of days with me. He prayed with me and said: 'You know, Bernard, I don't think God wants you anywhere else. You should just persevere and continue what you are doing, and he will show you the way out of this. He wants you playing golf and he wants you playing golf successfully, so you can reach out to other people and hopefully be a good example to others.'"

Langer stuck with his game and again rose to be among the top ten golfers in the world. As his words suggests, his faith in God has been instrumental in helping not only his golfing career, but also his life. "I was very fortunate to grow up in a religious home," he explains. "Both my parents believed in God. I went to church everyday, not just Sunday. I was an altar boy for seven years. This really laid the foundation for my Christian belief later on. I believed all my life in God. I was in a way very religious, but just never really had that personal relationship with Jesus Christ which is so important."

The turning point in Bernard's faith came shortly after the 1985 US Masters. "My priorities were golf, golf and more golf, then myself - and finally a little time with my wife. Every now and then prayed and went to church. But if my golf game was not good, my whole life was miserable and I made everyone around me miserable.

"I always thought I was doing all the right things. I always believed in God, I just didn't have this personal relationship. The week after I won the Masters, Bobby Clampett invited me to a Bible study. For the first time in my life I heard I needed to be reborn. He showed me Jesus' words: 'Truly, truly I say to you unless one is born again, he cannot see the kingdom of God' (John 3:3). But surely at the age of twenty-eight, I could not be born again.

"I had achieved basically everything I ever wanted to achieve. I was higher than I ever even could have dreamt of. I had a young, beautiful wife, all the money, I was number one in the golfing world, and yet when I woke up there was something missing. There was a void in my life and I realised I didn't know where I was going when this life here on earth was over.

"I then heard I could never get to heaven by my own deeds or by my own works, that I just have to trust Jesus Christ, that he died for my sins, and that this was the only way to get there. He has made sufficient payment for me and I should just accept him and put him on the throne of my life. That really got me going. Then I got myself a Bible, which I never had when I grew up, and started reading his word, growing and fellowshipping with other believers.

"After understanding that God loved me so much he sent his only Son, it was natural for me to ask the Lord into my life. Since then, I have seen tremendous changes in my life, my marriage and my whole outlook. My priorities have changed: now its God first, family second and then my career. I believe when your priorities are right, everything is managed better.

"Everyday, we have to make many decisions, but the most important decision we will ever make is who we believe Jesus is. We either accept him or reject him. Jesus himself said: 'You are either for me or against me.' There is no in-between."

Growing up, Bernard believed in God but really didn't know the Bible. "I heard small messages from the Bible in the sermons, but I never had my own Bible and I never had this personal relationship with God. I thought that hopefully I would get to heaven by my good deeds and then I will meet God. I never knew I could have this relationship right here in this world.

"Jesus said, 'I am the way, the truth, and the life, and no one gets to the father but through me.' Now if you realise what this means, you've got to stop, think about this for a second, and then turn around and focus on what you're doing in this world. No one in this world is good enough to get to heaven by their own deeds - not one - but, at the same time, no one is bad so they can't be saved by Jesus Christ."

Bernard Langer's faith has fundamentally changed his life and, in retrospect, he adds: "I believe it might take more faith not to believe in Jesus Christ than it takes to believe in him."

GAVIN PEACOCK

IN HIS BLOOD

Football is in Gavin Peacock's blood, his father playing over 500 games for English side Charlton Athletic. The midfielder turned professional straight from high school, joining Queens Park Rangers the day after his seventeenth birthday. He has also represented England at under-nineteen level, including a tour of Brazil. Even his wedding was sandwiched by football, playing for Bournemouth on Saturday, marrying Amanda on Sunday and reporting for training on Monday morning.

Most of Gavin's childhood memories involve football. "It was all I ever thought of doing," he says. "My dad used to position footballs strategically around the garden so that I couldn't help but bump into one and kick it. He encouraged me, but never pushed me into it. With him being a player at Charlton for seventeen years I was brought up in a footballing family and with football all around me."

The Englishman's earliest football memory is of his first goal, slotted for his school team. "A ball came across. I was in the six yard box and stuck my leg out. It went in off my knee, but it was a goal."

The Peacock family moved to America for two years when Gavin was eleven. After returning, Gavin recalls watching a schoolboy international between England and Scotland. His father, Keith, turned to him and said, "That could be you next year."

Gavin just laughed, but the following season found himself playing for his nation at Wembley. "You play for England on the Saturday and think you have made it," he says, "but there is nothing like going back to school on Monday and doing a maths exam to bring you back to earth."

Having played for England, Gavin was wanted by a number of professional clubs. Eventually he decided on QPR, partly because their manager was the highly respected coach, Terry Venables, and also because the club had a reputation for giving young players a chance.

Unfortunately the teenager struggled at Rangers, playing only a few games in the first team. At 19, he decided to drop down a division to gain experience and transferred to Gillingham. The club's manager was none other than Keith Peacock, and the deal was sealed between cornflakes and toast one morning.

Gavin flourished at Gillingham, scoring eleven goals in his sixty-nine league appearances. In 1989, the midfielder moved on to AFC Bournemouth, but his big break came when he signed with Newcastle the following year for £275,000.

Newcastle United was then a sleeping giant, a club with a great tradition, in a football-mad city, but languishing towards the bottom of the first division. It was also a kind of homecoming for Gavin as his father's roots were very much in England's northeast.

The club continued to struggle. Manager Jim Smith was replaced by Ossie Ardiles, the 1978 World Cup winner with Argentina and a legend at Tottenham. Ultimately he too paid the price, and Kevin Keegan was appointed.

Even in the early unsuccessful days Gavin was amazed how football-mad the city was. Driving around the city in his sponsored car he was a celebrity. If he and his wife ate in a restaurant they were aware of being watched, if not asked about the team's last game. Whenever he turned up for training or at St James' Park, fans mobbed him for autographs and photos.

"When I went to Newcastle I could not believe it," Peacock says. "It was my first taste of the big time. Although I had been with QPR when they were at the top, it was nothing like what I experienced at Newcastle. I could not believe the amount of press and cameras that were there waiting. Then it got bigger and bigger, especially when Kevin Keegan became manager. In my last season there, we were playing in front of 30,000 every home game.

"I remember one game away at Peterborough. I think the capacity was something like 14,000 and we had 7,000 Newcastle supporters. The passion and connection I made with those fans was something special to me. The three and a half years I was there were special times."

The enthusiastic support of the Newcastle fans had many effects. "Obviously pressure comes with the adulation," he says. "The bigger club, the more passion involved. You have to learn to handle it."

In 1993, Gavin captained Newcastle to the First Division title as the team earned promotion to the top division. That season he was also selected to the English First Division All Star team that played the Italian Serie B side, and was named Man-of-the-Match. The manager of the All Star team was Glenn Hoddle, then player/manager of Swindon Town.

Hoddle was already impressed with Peacock after he scored his best goal of that season during Newcastle's league game against Swindon Town. He controlled a long pass, flicked it up with one foot and volleyed it home with the other.

As the 1992-93 season ended, Newcastle United was promoted to the Premier League. Hoddle's Swindon Town was also promoted through the play-offs. Glenn and Gavin were preparing with their respective clubs, but before the new season started Glenn became manager of Chelsea, and Gavin was his first signing for £1.25 million. The twenty-five-year-old left Newcastle having found the back of the net forty-seven times in his 117 appearances.

Things were good for the man from Eltham, but Gavin had learnt to take nothing for granted in football. "You have to keep a level head," he says. "If you get carried away, football throws you from one extreme to another. Within a week you could be up at the top doing well, then two games later you're out of the team. You have to maintain a level head about it and, of course, my faith helps me in that.

"God gives me my self-worth, my value. I am a Christian first and then a footballer. In Matthew 6:34, Jesus says, 'Do not worry about tomorrow, for tomorrow will worry about itself. Each day has enough trouble of its own.' The idea of not worrying about tomorrow is so apt for the football world because you can't tell what is going to happen in the next training session, let alone in the next few weeks or years, which is such a long time in football. To know God has it all in hand and that Jesus tells me not to worry is great."

Gavin grew up being taught to tell right from wrong, but God did not have much place in his thinking. When his mother, Lesley, started going to church, Gavin gradually began to take notice. "I saw the change in her life and wondered what it was all about, so I went along. I believed in God, but he was up there somewhere. He was distant. For the first time I realised Jesus is around us all the time. He is here with us now and that reality of knowing Christ really came home to me, so I made a commitment to follow Jesus."

If Newcastle in 1990 was a sleeping giant, then so was Chelsea in 1993, a club that had not won a trophy since the FA Cup in 1970. With Hoddle as player/manager there was a buzz about the place. Gavin took to the premiership without difficulty.

In September he found himself opposing Manchester United at Stamford Bridge. Chelsea won one-nil, and Gavin scored. "I nicked the ball over Peter Schmeichel. It was the start of my Chelsea career. I had only played three or four games and I'd got Manchester United. I could not believe it. In the early part of my career I had been playing against lower, possibly first division opposition. Now I was playing Premier League against Manchester United and I scored the winner."

Not content with one victory over England's premier club, Chelsea repeated the feat at Old Trafford the following February. When Mark Stein headed on, Gavin was first to the ball and lobbed it over Schmeichel. One-nil to Chelsea for the second time, and Gavin again scored the winner.

That year Chelsea reached the Cup final with Gavin scoring six goals in the cup run. In the sixth round Gavin scored the only goal against the Wolves to take Chelsea into a semi-final against Luton Town, a game that Gavin will never forget.

"It was at Wembley. We won two-nil and I scored both goals. From a personal point of view that was my favourite game, because we played at Wembley and it was the first time Chelsea got there for so many years."

To win the cup Chelsea needed to beat Manchester United. An incident in the first half had people wondering whether lightning could strike three times. "We were doing well. At one stage I got hold of the ball outside the box, knocked it on to my left foot and hit it. I thought, 'This is going in.' It dipped over Schmeichel's hand and hit the bar." Unfortunately it was not Chelsea's day, the ball hit the bar and Manchester United went on to win four-nil.

Another of Gavin's proudest memories from his time at Chelsea was a Premier League hat-trick against Middlesbrough.

After three years Glenn Hoddle became manager of England, and Ruud Gullit became manager in his place. Despite being a regular member of the First Team squad at Stamford Bridge, Gavin found himself squeezed out by an influx of foreign imports. Making fewer appearances, he decided to return to QPR in late 1996. There he continues to play, also making a brief reappearance in the Premier League in late 2001 on loan to Charlton.

As a seasoned professional, Gavin has learnt how to deal with situations on and off the field. On tour there can be opportunities and temptations to handle. "I have been on many trips and there is nothing wrong with going out, having a drink and just being with the lads. As a Christian we all know where to draw the line and I think that would be fairly obvious. You would not go any further than that.

"I have always made that my standard and I have never had a problem dealing with it. Certainly over my career I have been very clear about what I would and would not do. All the lads at the clubs I have been at have known that."

The secret is keeping Christ at the centre, and everything else in perspective. "My faith runs through my whole life. It strengthens me as a person and I have carried that over into whatever I am doing. Whether that is football, just being at home, my marriage or relationships with other people, my faith has helped me. Focusing on God and putting my trust and values in him, has helped me remember that football is not the be-all and end-all - although it is important and is my job. God is a constant and he will be there when football has gone."

This chapter was written by Stuart Weir

SHAUN POLLOCK

IN THE GENES

In South Africa the Pollock name is synonymous with cricket, and Shaun Pollock continues to make that association stronger. His uncle, Graeme, averaged 60.97 to be one of the game's great batsman, while his father, Peter, averaged more than twenty with the bat and took 116 Test wickets with the ball.

"As long as I can remember I was playing cricket," Shaun says, "even if it was just in the backyard. Obviously the family was a cricket family, so there were a lot of genes that pushed me that way. I wanted to do what my father and the rest of the family were doing. My uncle only gave up in 1986. I used to watch him play in provincial games. To see one of your family out there playing was an inspiration. I always talked cricket with my father. He gave up in 1973, which was the year I was born, so I never saw him play. They both had a big influence on me wanting to play cricket, but it wasn't always smooth going because we didn't have international cricket when I was growing up. I didn't think I could play cricket as a profession. Luckily the doors opened up after that."

Since making his Test debut against England in November 1995, Shaun has more than lived up to the Pollock name. When he claimed the wicket of Sri Lankan Nuwan Zoysa in December 2000, Pollock became the only the second South African to take 200 Test wickets, and the thirty-seventh in Test history.

Pollock has also performed in the One-Day arena. In March 1999, he completed the 1000 run, 100 wicket double in the least number of matches in history. Pollock took sixty-eight games to reach the target, bettering Ian Botham (seventy-five), Kapil Dev (seventy-seven) and Richard Hadlee (seventy-nine). Shaun was also the youngest player to complete the double and did it in the shortest career span, both records previous held by Australian captain Steve Waugh. Pollock was twenty-five years and 253 days old, bettering Waugh by thirty-one days, and his career span was three years and seventy-seven days, almost two years better than Waugh.

In April 2001, Shaun also completed the rare double of 2000 Test runs and 200 Test wickets. Pollock reached the landmark with a massive six in the fifth test against the West Indies at Sabina Park. Playing in his fifty-sixth test, he is only the eight cricketer to complete the double and the fifth quickest to do so.

Despite these achievements, Pollock says his debut was the highlight of his career. "It's something I'd always dreamt of," he says. "The experience won't easily be forgotten. Victory at the Commonwealth Games, captaining South Africa for the first time, my maiden Test century and a five wicket haul to win an away series against Pakistan are also some of my most memorable moments."

Shaun's maiden Test century came two matches after taking his 200th wicket, and confirmed his status as an all-rounder. Batting partner Neil McKenzie said of the innings, "It was like a highlights package all by itself."

Pollock's century came off ninety-five balls. When he finally departed on 111, he had hit sixteen fours and three sixes. "I can't explain it," Pollock said afterwards, "I tried a couple of cuts and the ball came off the bat sweetly and went for four. It was just one of those days."

Shaun was the Man-of-the-Match in that innings and seven run victory to South Africa, and also picked up the honour against Australia in January 1998 when he bowled a career best seven for eighty-seven.

Peter Roebuck wrote in the *Sydney Morning Herald*: "Shaun Pollock has produced one of the gamest fast bowling efforts it has been my privilege to watch. It was a performance of which any cricketer can be proud. Quite simply he bowled his heart out. Given the responsibility of leading the attack, he bowled until his shirt was wringing wet – then he bowled some more."

Shaun has also performed at county level in England. "I went to play a season with Warwickshire," he says. "In my debut match I was pretty nervous. Everyone was looking to the new pro to see how he would perform. I went out there, and in my fourth over I got four wickets in four balls. That relaxed me."

Pollock became the South African captain in April 2000, after the dismissal of Hansie Cronje in one of cricket's darkest moments. "It was an awkward time in South African cricket," he says. "I didn't anticipate any overnight changes in responsibility, but fortunately I had support from both team and management. To a large degree the South African public had a lot of sympathy for the side and allowed us a honeymoon period or sorts. Amidst the drama, the best we could do was to focus on the game.

"The most trying aspect of being a captain is simultaneously managing the team's performance as well as your own. During pressure times I find it a great help to concentrate on the immediate task at hand, rather than letting the enormity of the situation overwhelm me. There is also a challenge in ensuring we as a team collectively get the best result from what are effectively twelve individual characters. It's interesting that although modern books and seminars talk about contemporary ideals of leadership, these are often based on simple Biblical principles."

Cronje's fall shocked the world, and hit Pollock particularly hard because the former captain was a fellow Christian. "The scandal really illustrated that every one of us is fallible," Shaun says. As a Christian, Pollock knows all people make mistakes and need God's forgiveness. That is why God sent his son to take the punishment for sin, so the world could be reconciled with God.

Pollock became a Christian at fifteen, under the influence of his parents. "We used to have wild parties," he says. "Our family was basically the regular family, throwing parties, drinking, that sort of stuff. There was not much real love shown.

"Then my mother and father became Christians. I saw the change in their lives, the love they started to give, and the support, and how everything changed. That was the main reason for me becoming a Christian."

Shaun believes being a Christian helps him on the field. "It gives you a level head. When you have good performances and when you have bad performances, you can put them into perspective. In cricket there are more downs than ups. Every time you go out you want to score a hundred, every time you go out to bowl you want to take five wickets, and that very rarely happens. There are a lot of downs, and part of cricket is to pick yourself up and keep going forward. Being a Christian helps keep things in perspective. A lot of people have a bad game and for the rest of the week they're down, but I think being a Christian you can go to the Bible and pray. It picks you up much quicker, and you can continue on to the next game."

Pollock denies the accusation that Christians are soft. "When you're out in the field," he says, "you've got to be as hard as the next chap. Some people think Christians are soft, but I think you've got to realise we're just the same as any other person on the cricket field, and we play just as hard when we're out there. Off the field we have a different perspective, but on the field we're as hard as the next person."

Shaun also wishes to use his talents on the field to impact on people's lives off the field. "God has given me a talent," he says, "and I'm there to use my talent to further his kingdom. I think you've been given the talent by him, and it's not there to be abused, but you must use it so you can touch other people's lives."

The greatest way in which Pollock wants to touch other people's lives is to help them enter into a relationship with God. "A lot of people look for the true meaning of life," he says. "After winning a cricket series or something, you tend to ask, 'What's the big deal?' Two days later the adrenaline rush has worn off, and if you think about that – and a lot of people do – they think to themselves, 'What's the big deal?' They're looking for meaning in life, and the answer is definitely Christianity. With the Lord in your life, your life takes on a whole new meaning.

"Christianity is the way to go. Some people talk about religion, but Christianity is more real to me because you can have a direct relationship with Christ – you don't have to go the religion route."

Despite his cricket successes, things don't always go Shaun's way. One match stands out as being more disappointing than all the others - the tied World Cup semi-final in 1999 against Australia. With one run needed to win off the last four balls, after Lance Klusener had hit fifteen from the previous four, the Australian team moved in around Klusener. Their only hope was to take South Africa's last wicket and tie the match, causing them to go through to the final as they were higher on the table. The South Africans tried for a single, but were denied. Damien Fleming bowled the fourth ball of the last over. Klusener hit it back down the wicket and began running.

However, Allan Donald stood frozen at the other end. When he realised what was happening he dropped his bat and began running, but it was too late as the Australians had fielded the ball to Adam Gilchrist who removed the bails. South Africa was all out for 213, tying with Australia's score - the first time a tie had occurred in World Cup history - and out of the World Cup.

Pollock was South Africa's finest player, taking five wickets for thirty-six runs and adding twenty with the bat off just fourteen balls, but it wasn't enough. "As a sportsperson you're always going to go through ups and downs," he says. "I enjoy the message of the popular poem Footprints. It's about how a chap looks back at his life and there are two sets of footprints at times. Then when he's really struggling there's only one set of footprints. He questions the Lord and says to him, 'Now listen, what's going on here? How come at my hardest times you left me alone?' And the Lord answers, 'It was at those times I carried you.'

"It's a constant reminder that the Lord is there for each of us in good times and bad, and we should learn to depend on him always. Although hard work and dedication will reap you rewards in your chosen career, these rewards are very short lived. Through the same commitment and devotion to the Lord Jesus Christ you can reap the far greater reward of eternal life."

JONTY RHODES

THE INSIDE EDGE

A single moment during the 1992 Cricket World Cup changed the course of Jonty Rhodes' life. Fielding on the Gabba in Brisbane, Australia, the South African catapulted himself from relative obscurity to fame, dive-bombing the stumps to dismiss Pakistani batsman Inzamam-ul-Haq.

"I was not aiming at the stumps," Jonty says, recalling the incident, which helped South Africa snatch victory from Pakistan. "I didn't have the opportunity to do so. For the first time I felt very tense. Suddenly, I thought I might miss the stumps and anything at that stage would have been unpardonable. I saw Inzamam getting back much faster than I had imagined. I had to hit the stumps faster than him and the only way I thought was through the air."

The photo of Jonty parallel to the ground, crashing through the stumps, found its way onto the front page of most newspapers around the cricketing world. Back in South Africa shirts were printed, reading: "It's a bird. It's a plane. No, it's Jonty." Outside the dressing-room after the game, hundreds of South African supporters gathered chanting, "We want Jonty, we want Jonty."

"It changed my life," Jonty adds, "from being a really obscure person, quiet and deeply hidden - no one really knew who Jonty Rhodes was, I came to the World Cup and no one expected me to even play - to all of a sudden being front page on most of the newspapers around the world where they play cricket."

The world was amazed, but nothing surprised those who had seen Jonty in action before. In 1990, the South African was playing at home for Natal against Transvaal. "Richard Snell was bowling to me," he explains. "We needed seven runs to win off the last ball." In cricket, even if you hit the ball out of the ground you only get six runs, so a win seemed impossible. "He bowled me a no-ball which I hit for six, and then the extra ball I hit for four. So I scored ten off one ball to win the match."

Reflecting on this Jonty adds, "It has been my attitude throughout my cricketing career that you never give up until the last ball is bowled, because you never know what might happen."

Regarded as one of the game's finer fielders, Jonty has earned this accolade through seemingly endless dives, catches and run-outs. One of his finest days in the field was in Bombay, India, in late-1993. After his team set a modest total of 180, the only way to win was with an exceptional effort in the field. Jonty gave even better. In a Man-of-the-Match performance, Rhodes took a world record five catches, including an amazing leap to dismiss Anderson Cummins that left the crowd in stunned disbelief. The West Indies crumbled to all-out for 139; South Africa the victors.

Such moments in the field have lead to the birth of a common expression in cricketing circles: "Two thirds of the world is covered by water, the rest by Jonty Rhodes."

Most cricketers would be happy to retire having achieved just one of these feats. However, for Rhodes none of them is even his career highlight. "The best moment for me in cricket was the first Test hundred I scored," he says, remembering his 101 not-out in Moratuwa, Sri Lanka, in August 1993. During the inaugural Test match between South Africa and Sri Lanka, the tourists were chasing a fourth innings total of 365 off 115 overs. From a dire 138 for six, Rhodes led an inspired revival to hold the team together until the end of play.

"All the newspapers before we left South Africa said, 'Jonty Rhodes shouldn't play in the test because he can't play spin.' In the first test match, I got one hundred not out. It helped the side save the game; we got a draw. That for me was the most satisfying."

Rhodes also claimed the South African record for the fastest Test century, in terms of balls faced, for a superb 103 not-out against the West Indies in January 1999. His innings lasted ninety-five deliveries and included six sixes and eight fours. In Jonty's typical humble and humorous manner, he didn't even realise he had broken a record. "The guys told me when I got back to the dressing room," he says. "If I'd beaten a guy like Barry Richards, I'd have been quite chuffed, but I'm actually quite embarrassed that it's Klusener. People call him a slogger and now I've gone and broken his record. What will people call me?"

Jonty's list of highlights could go on: his return to form with a career best 117 against England at Lord's in 1998; or his world record fourth wicket partnership of 232 with Daryll Cullinan against Pakistan in 1996, scoring his highest One-Day score of 121 off just 114 balls; or the 2001-02 season against Australia and New Zealand where he finished the One-Day series with the most runs (345), highest average (57.50) and highest score (107 not out), hitting his 5,000 career run along the way; or the following One-Day series against Australia where he again topped the scoring with 338 runs at 67.60.

The cricketer's abilities have earned him respect around the world. Former Australian captain Mark Taylor says: "Jonty Rhodes is a live wire - especially in the field where he ranks with the world's best. Nobody enjoys the game more than Jonty." To these sentiments current Australian Test captain Steve Waugh adds: "Jonty is a very good player and has the ability to lift others around him. He's the key to their side whenever they are on the park. Even when he is a twelfth man, he does all sorts of little things to help out. He's very unselfish and sets an example to the rest of the team, lifting the team as a whole. He always seems happy, which is important in a team situation. He has plenty of energy and is the best fielder in the world. As a batter, he's very capable at the top level."

Jonty is an extraordinary cricketer, but cricket is not his primary motivation in life. "Cricket is something I have loved to play since I was big enough to hold a bat," he says, "but for me success is not merely measured in the number of games we win or how many runs I score. I know the Lord is using me as a witness regardless of my average and success. I want to be the best I can be for my God. After all, cricket is just a game." Jonty always considered himself to be a Christian. He had a Christian background, went to church every Christmas and Easter, and occasionally went to Sunday School and youth group. In 1989, however, after meeting Kate McCarthy, who would later become his wife, the cricketer realised something was missing.

"She had something which I envied," he says. "She had such a close relationship with God that every minute of the day she knew she was in the Lord's presence. I had a very up and down personality. When I was up, I was really high and when I was down, I was pretty down on myself. That all changed when I gave my life to God, because I realised I was being successful by just being there for the Lord and being a witness for him. It didn't depend on me scoring a hundred or taking catches or getting run-outs. It all depended on me being there for God and him using me.

"Whatever success you achieve, whatever material wealth you achieve, there is always something missing - and that something is the Holy Spirit. I might not have scored more runs now I'm a Christian, I might not of taken more catches or got more run-outs because I am Christian - or made more money - but I am satisfied in my heart and that is what is important. Whatever you gain, whatever records you attain, they're going to be left behind. It's what you've got in your heart that is going to be taken with you."

During the 1992 World Cup where Rhodes performed his remarkable run-out, he also experienced what he considers the worst day in his cricketing career. In what was possibly the most controversial day in cricket since the "underarm" incident in 1981, South Africa was competing against England for a berth in the World Cup final. With thirteen balls to be bowled, rain started falling on the Sydney Cricket Ground. The South Africans needed twenty-two runs to exceed the English total of 252, a difficult but possible task. After seventeen minutes delay, the scoreboard announced the revised requirement: twenty-two runs from seven deliveries. The crowd began jeering; immediately the umpires met to confer. The scoreboard registered an adjustment: twenty-one runs, one ball. The dream of a World Cup victory was over. South African batsman Brian McMillan faced the delivery, pushing the ball to mid-wicket for a single. Finishing the run, he walked off the ground disgusted, South Africa left nineteen runs shy of their opponent's total and out of the World Cup.

In sport as in life, there are ups and downs and Jonty has experienced both, but his faith helps him keep going. "Being a Christian doesn't guarantee you a smooth ride. You know every Christian is faced with temptations; every Christian is faced with difficulties. I was told once by a good friend, 'If you aren't facing difficulties in your life, you're not being a very effective Christian. Because if you're not being effective for God, Satan is not going to bother you.' If you've got a strong relationship with the Lord and you're doing his work, Satan doesn't like it - and you're going to encounter pitfalls.

"There are quite a few non-Christian guys in the team and I quite often wonder how they cope with all the pressures. International cricket is very stressful. It might not look like it -

you travel the world, you see some wonderful places and you play in some beautiful settings - but it is stressful. I wonder how the guys who don't have the Lord as the centre of their life cope with that. I know that whatever I'm doing, I'm not doing it by myself, I'm not trying to do it on my own strength - God is there and he's the one giving me all the strength.

"By knowing God is in control of every game and every day of my life, there's no pressure on me to perform. Whatever I do, I'm being successful because the Lord is using me as a witness. Be it with a hundred or fifteen in a One-Day game, run-outs and catches - nothing. Just by being there, I am being successful. It takes a lot of pressure off me. The Lord is using me in every situation, so I don't have to perform every time I go out there. I can go out there and just be Jonty Rhodes - and give the Lord my best."

The South African's days in Test cricket are over, announcing his retirement in November 2000 so he could spend more time with his wife and new child. In his fifty-two tests he scored 2532 runs at an average of 35.66, including three centuries and a high score of 117. Despite being out of Test cricket, Jonty still plans to continue in the One-Day side until the 2003 World Cup.

GLYNDYN RINGROSE

ON THE RISE

Catching wind-chopped waves in a dugout canoe in the Solomon Islands was the beginning of Glyndyn Ringrose's attraction to surfing, an attraction that has seen him rise through the ranks of his sport to compete against the world's elite.

Born in the island nation of Vanuatu, in the South Pacific, surf is very much in his blood. Glyndyn's parents were missionaries from New Zealand, and worked in Vanuatu until he was three. The family then moved to Fiji for a few years, and then onto the Solomon Islands.

Ringrose remembers, "That was the most awesome time of my growing up in the tropics. I was just running around having a ball. I was hanging out with the islanders, having a great time, really enjoying life. We had our own little canoes and went fishing on them. When a bit of wind started blowing, we'd catch the wind-chop running down the lagoon. That was my first taste of surfing - the speed and the rush you get out of a wave. I also saw a photo of someone dropping into a wave on a surfboard when I lived there, and I thought, 'Wow, I'd love to do that.'

"Mum and dad moved to Australia when I was ten. As soon as I got to Australia, we moved to Port Macquarie - we just went straight to the water. We bought little foam surfboards that we used to go out and charge on. We had a great time. I was so keen on surfing that every chance I had I was out there having a good time. It was such a natural rush.

"I really enjoy going surfing, and I enjoy the environment. If I haven't surfed for a day or two I feel quite dirty. I feel like I need to surf to wash myself. Surfing is a very fulfilling sport, you're out in the ocean and anything can happen. It is such a beautiful environment to be in."

Glyndyn's rise in competitive surfing didn't begin until he moved to Phillip Island off the south coast of Australia. "It's been a step by step thing for me," he says. "I never really competed as a junior, but when I moved to Phillip Island I started doing the Boardriders contests down there. After Boardriders, I went into the State rounds and then got into a few Aussie titles. I then started on the Australian Championship Circuit (ACC) and did ok in that.

"When I was doing the ACC, I moved onto the World Qualifying Series (WQS) and in the first year finished something like 250th. The next year I finished sixty-eighth. Then in 1998 I finished seventeenth, which qualified me for the 1999 World Championship Tour (WCT). It was a gradual increase all the way up, step by step by step."

1998 was an amazing year for Glyndyn in the WQS, as he tried to surf his way in to the WCT. "I started the year thinking I would like to make the forty-four. I was really focused for the job, but never dreamt I would. I knew I was good enough, but it was a matter of getting the right waves and having the right fortune."

Glyndyn's success began with a fourth place in the Copa D'Onofrioi Pro in Peru. Then in Western Australia he added a ninth in the Coca-Cola Masters at Margaret River. But it wasn't until reaching Europe that he really began to climb up the rankings ladder.

Surfing in Anglet, France, in the O'Neil Surf Challenge, Glyndyn recorded the highest scoring wave in the final, finishing second. He then crossed the channel to win the Virgin Cola Intersurf Pro in England. Ringrose was rising, and his dreams of making the end of year cut were being realised.

He added another second at the Headworx Surf Classic in Spain, and then a seventh in Portugal at the Buondi Sintra Pro. "All these were in a row," he remembers. "I went from sixtieth to fifth in the WQS rankings."

The islander's form waned as the series moved to South America, until the last event when he tamed the unpredictable Brazilian beach breaks to make the final of the Marathon Pro in Rio de Janeiro. "Every heat, I couldn't believe it, I got a good barrel," he says. "Every heat I got one. No one else got a barrel in every heat - no one hardly got a barrel in the whole contest."

Rolling on from South America, Glyndyn moved to the final location of the 1998 WQS - the Rip Curl World Cup at Sunset, Hawaii. "I was right on the borderline," he says. "At that stage the top eighteen got onto the WCT, and I was ranked seventeenth."

Managing to hold his seventeenth place after some tight competition at Sunset, Ringrose made it onto the WCT - securing his position at the last possible moment.

Reflecting on his 1998 successes, he concedes, "There were so many heats where it had been so close, where I'd fallen off three waves in a row. All of a sudden I'd get an eight-pointer with seconds to go and get knocked through the heat. There's no way I'd be where I am without the 'Big Man Upstairs'."

Glyndyn first learnt about God from his parents while they were doing missionary work in the Pacific. "My parents brought me up believing in Jesus," he says, "and believing he died for us and took our sins. I always knew as a child he was real, and knew he would answer my prayers. I felt that connection between him and I.

"As I grew up through my teens I lost my way a bit. It's really only been since getting married that I've got that connection back again. My wife, Kate, and I spend time together reading the Bible and learning more."

Through studying the Bible, the surfer has become sure about what he believes. "I believe that Jesus was God on earth. He came and lived a perfect life and never did anything wrong. Yet he was killed for us and then resurrected. He died for our sins. All we need to do is ask him for forgiveness and our sins are gone. We have to turn our lives over to him. Whatever we do, there is a God out there and he is watching. All we need to do is call on him."

Travelling the world, visiting every continent except Antarctica, with the WQS and the WCT is harder than most people would expect. "The last couple of years have been challenging," he says. "I've needed God's help to get me through it. Just getting visas usually takes a small miracle. Then you travel to strange destinations you have never been to before. You arrive in the middle of the night with a piece of paper with the name of a beach on it. There are different languages to come to terms with, different cultures, laws and religions. It's a lot to deal with, especially when you are travelling on your own. Then on top of that I usually have to do well in a contest to make enough money to get to the next destination. It takes a lot of faith, and a lot of commitment. It hasn't been easy.

"My constant prayer is, 'Lord, help me at this next destination. I don't know what's going to happen or how I'm going to get around. Help me with the uncertainties. Help me as I'm out of my comfort zone.' I've learnt that my faith would never develop if I remained in my comfort zone. I've learnt to trust God as I place myself in positions where I have no alternative but to trust him."

One of the hardest times for Glyndyn was in Brazil in 1997. Small wave surfing is his Achilles heel, and that is basically what Brazil is - one big small wave. After losing successive competitions in either the first or second heat, his confidence sunk.

"When you're on a losing streak you psychologically get ripped apart. I lost all my confidence in Brazil. In the last contest I paddled out feeling totally defeated before the heat even started. I couldn't even figure out where I was going to sit to catch waves. I was an emotional wreck. My confidence was at an all time low.

"All these things kept building and building. I felt really lost. I was missing Kate and was really lonely. I lost my first heat and then as I was leaving the water this guy came up to me and said, 'You haven't paid for the contest.' I had paid, but he was demanding I pay another US$100 for the entry fee. I only had about $300 at this stage and tried to explain that I needed all my money to get home. He demanded I pay it, so I gave him the money. By this stage I was shattered. I was worn out. I just wanted to go home, I'd had enough of the tour."

Fortunately, adversity like this, along with his faith, has slowly helped him come to terms with the uncertainties of competing on the world tour. "There will always be lows you need to endure, but it's faith that gets you through. When you're winning you feel so confident, it's like nothing can touch you. That is what it was like for me in Europe in 1998. Then I went to Brazil and didn't do very well in the first three contests. Suddenly I felt all this on me again. I was starting to get depressed; the same feelings were coming back from 1997. I got to Rio for the fourth contest and was praying, 'Please help me here Lord.'

"I felt good before the contest and then my ear blocked up with water. Two hours before my first heat I was in hospital getting my ear flushed out. I got back with just enough time to paddle out for my heat. I was flustered about it. Again I just asked God to calm me down and set me straight. I had putty in one ear and the other was unblocked. I ended up making the final. It felt like a miracle."

As a Christian within the surfing world, Glyndyn believes his surfing is his ministry. "God has put me there for a reason," he says, "and that is to share with others about him. I see so many who live without God and there is a kind of emptiness, there is a longing for something, but they don't know what it is.

"For most surfers there is an almost spiritual side to surfing. A lot of surfers believe in God, or in a spiritual being. I get quite a few opportunities on tour to share my faith with others. The guys are searching, they're having a hard time, they're away from home, and they're not in their comfort zone. They tend to come to me and ask why I'm not having all these problems, what have I got that they haven't. A lot of them are asking questions.

"Some guys think surfing is going to fulfill all their dreams, they're going to go to the top and make plenty of money. But only one thing can bring ultimate fulfillment, and that is a relationship with God through believing in Jesus Christ."

Surfing on the WCT brought both success and disappointment, one of the highs came in the Tahiti Pro at Teahupoo in 1999. "In my first heat," he remembers, "the waves were a solid eight to ten feet, and Jake Paterson dropped in on me. I took off inside of him - no one thought I was going to make the wave. I held my line, and we were both inside the tube. I was so deep I couldn't see my way out. I just held on and held on and held on, and travelled the whole length of the tube really deep. He came out, and then I came out. I scored a ten, and he scored an interference. It's really hard to score anything above an 8.5, and I got a ten. You've got to surf really well. I progressed through, and went all the way to the quarter finals."

Glyndyn's solid form continued throughout his first year. "I was twenty-seventh in the world. It was incredible. I didn't expect to be there. I just went step by step by step, and then I was there, surfing against the best in the world, and sometimes beating them. I was blown away."

Unfortunately Ringrose couldn't repeat his ranking in 2000, finishing outside the top twenty-eight that automatically requalify to the WCT for the following year. He also narrowly finished outside the top sixteen in the WQS that qualify, despite winning the Rio Marathon Surf WQS event at Barra de Tijuca in Brazil.

"I was struggling," he says. "I had a lot of last placings, and was saying to God, 'What's going on here? I really want to do your will, and be a champion for you.' It just wasn't happening. No matter what I prayed, or how hard I tried, it just didn't work. The Lord took me a step back and made me look and realise where I was, and what I was really there for. I'm not there for me, I'm there for him."

Ringrose believes he has grown through his time on the WCT. "God has taught me to be a stronger person spiritually," he says. "It's a struggle when you're away from church. I think he's also taught me never to get egotistical or proud."

Despite falling off the WCT, Glyndyn received the full support of his major sponsor, Quiksilver. It is paying for him to surf the WQS and earn his way back onto the WCT, while looking after the younger Quiksilver sponsored surfers.

"I achieved quite a few goals I set myself," he says, "and along the way I got to meet a lot of people and talk to them about God. I didn't quite achieve the goals I really wanted to, but I'm sure there are still a lot of things coming up."

DAVID ROBINSON

BEYOND THE RIM

Shooting hoops on the streets of Virginia is a long way from being named one of the National Basketball Association's (NBA) all time greatest players. David Robinson knows, he has walked that road.

Despite the journey beginning on the bench during his last high school year, it wasn't long before Robinson took his first step. "Right before the first game," he remembers, "the starting centre sprained his ankle, so I started. I played well enough that from that point on I played the rest of the season, even when he got better."

Upon finishing high school "The Admiral", as he came to be known, received a few minor offers to play basketball, but decided to follow his father's footsteps into the Navy. "I had pretty much decided I wanted to go to the Naval Academy. The recruiters complicated that a little bit, but not very much. I liked basketball, but was focused on going to the Naval Academy because I wanted the discipline and the education."

Fortunately, joining the academy didn't stop Robinson's playing days, it just decided the team. In his first season with Navy, he was 6 foot 4 inches (1.93m) and averaged 7.6 points per game. In his sophomore year, he realised his future lay in basketball. Remembering a game in which he tallied sixty-eight points and thirty-one rebounds he says, "That was the first time I got an idea of what I could do." By graduation, the All American had grown seven inches, picked up three Collegiate records, been named 1987 College Player of the Year and increased his average points per game to 28.2.

David Robinson was hot.

The San Antonio Spurs won the right to first pick in the 1987 NBA Draft and decided to go with Robinson, even though it meant two years of sleepless nights as he fulfilled his naval service commitment.

On schedule, the twenty-four-year-old rookie walked into the Spurs' line up in 1989. As one of the more gifted fresh bloods in recent years, Robinson proved to be worth the wait. The centre was integral to the Spurs' thirty-five-game turn-around on the previous season - the greatest in NBA history. That season, Robinson earned every NBA Rookie of the Month title, was the only rookie included in an All-Star side and was the obvious choice as NBA Rookie of the Year.

Robinson continued to dazzle the NBA. The three-time member of the "Dream Team" has won two Olympic Gold medals, been named to ten All-Star sides, became only the fourth player in NBA history to record a quadruple-double (34 points, 10 rebounds, 10 assists, and 10 blocked shots on February 17, 1994), clinched the 93-94 scoring crown by shooting seventy-one points on the last day of the season, and was named the NBA's Most Valuable Player for the 1994-1995 season.

In March 2002, with a free throw against Golden State in the third quarter, The Admiral scored his 20,000th point to a standing ovation. "When I was a rookie," he said after winning the match, "I was just a scared rookie looking to make something happen. To think thirteen years from then, here I am, looking at 20,000 points and being named one of the league's all-time top 50 players and having won a championship, you know it's unbelievable. I still don't think I have a grasp on what has been accomplished around here, along with the type of career I've had."

Of all Robinson's achievement, his seventy-one point game was something special. "Generally I don't get wrapped up in individual accomplishments. My primary focus is on the team. I try to win games and not worry about personal goals. I don't like getting too much hype. One time, however, there was an opportunity to win the NBA scoring title and I capitalised on it - with lots of help from my teammates.

"It came on the final day of the 1994 regular season. I was locked in a close duel with Shaquille O'Neal, who was playing for the Orlando Magic, for the scoring championship. Going into our final games, he was ahead by a fraction of a point. I needed to outscore O'Neal by four points to win the title. San Antonio was playing on the road against the Los Angeles Clippers, while Orlando was at home against the New Jersey Nets later that day.

"From the opening tip, I was hot. I scored the Spurs' first eighteen points. Once my teammates realised I had such a hot hand, they kept looking for me, trying to get me the ball. The Clippers, of course, were trying hard to stop me. They were fighting, clawing, bumping, grinding, and double and triple teaming me to try and keep me from scoring. I had the scratches and bruises to show for it. I went to the foul line twenty-five times that night.

"I really got rolling in the third period and scored nineteen points, giving me forty-three for the game. Even the Clippers' fans were cheering for me despite the fact that Los Angeles had a good shot at winning the game, trailing by only four after three quarters.

"The fourth quarter was remarkable. Despite tremendous pressure from the Clippers' defense, who knew the ball was going to me most of the time, I scored twenty-eight points. That gave me a total of seventy-one, a total that put me into some elite company. Only three other players - Wilt Chamberlain, David Thompson and Elgin Baylor - had scored as many as seventy points in an NBA game.

"After the game, which we won 112-97, I figured the scoring race was over. I didn't think Shaq would beat me. He didn't. O'Neal needed sixty-eight points against the Nets to take back the scoring lead, but finished with thirty-two.

"I was the scoring champion for the first time in my NBA career, an honour for which I owe much to my teammates. I couldn't have done it without them. Their unselfishness was a very positive thing. It was fun to be a part of such an accomplishment. That's why I rank that as the most memorable game of my career. I don't usually place a high priority on individual accomplishments, but that was different."

Scoring crown runner-up, Shaquille O'Neal sums up: "You can't stop a guy like David Robinson; you can only try to slow him down. He can take over a game any given night."

Robinson realised a dream in 1999 when he helped the Spurs win the NBA championship in five games over the New York Knicks, silencing the Madison Square Garden crowd. "It's just starting to soak in, and, boy, it's been a long journey. It's a joy. It's worth every minute of the journey," he said after the game.

"You know that one big goal I had, achieving that goal, has been met. Now I have to set new goals and new things. If this was easy though, it wouldn't be worth the journey. That's what makes it so special. You go through all those hard times, you get through all the creases and everything else, then you're able to finally get it done. It's satisfying."

Despite winning the championship, Robinson still maintained his level head. "We fought hard and did it the right way," he says. "The ring is nice, but it's too big and clunky to wear. It's going to sit on my shelf. If you think it's the ring or the trophy that's going to make you happy, you're sorely mistaken.

"My life would not be any less complete had I not won the championship. That's the way your life should be. Our job is to make the most of what we have. That's all you can do."

The Spurs victory can largely be attributed to Tim Duncan joining the team in 1997-98. Slumping during the previous season – mainly because Robinson missed most of it through injury - earned San Antonio a first round pick in the 1997 NBA Draft, where they chose Duncan. Ironically, Robinson's injury led to the fulfilling of his basketball dream.

"Everything works for a reason," he says, remembering back to 1996-97 where he played just six games. "That was a hard season. The season before we had a pretty good team, we won over fifty games. It was basically the same team, except I was sitting on the bench. I was disappointed we weren't able to play better than we did. Plus that combined with me worrying about my back and whether I'd be able to run up and down the court again and help this team. So it was a very tough season. That was pretty much the low point."

David Robinson is a basketball success story, but one of his greatest achievements is largely unknown. Through years of sacrifice and dedication, Robinson has become one of the league's all-time leading players in assists – not in terms of passes leading to baskets, but in terms of help given others.

"You are the light of the world. A city set on a hill cannot be hidden," reads Matthew 5:14. Inspired by this verse, David and his wife, Valerie, established the David Robinson Foundation in late 1992.

"We wanted to emulate what Jesus did in his community and so that's our scripture," says David, "that you are the light of the world and you cannot hide under a lampshade. You sit up on top of the hill so you can touch everybody.

"That was the idea with our foundation – to be a light, to be an example and touch as many lives as we can. It's been a wonderful experience. We've really enjoyed the ministry."

The all-time Olympic highest scorer loves in response to the love he has been shown. "I didn't have a lot to do with being seven-foot one-inch," he says. "That was a gift. My talent as a basketball player was a gift. This is my opportunity to give back. My whole motivation is to please God, to be responsible to him. God has given me more than I ever hoped for, so it's my responsibility to give back."

Through the foundation, Robinson has given generously to many in need, including food for the hungry and college scholarships for students. But in 1997 he raised the bar of giving among professional athletes to unprecedented heights. That year Robinson donated US$5 million to establish a school on the east side of San Antonio, in one of the city's poorest areas, named the Carver Academy.

Upon learning of the donation, NBA Commissioner David Stern said, "David's $5 million pledge stands out as one of the most extraordinary in all of sports." For his generosity, Robinson was awarded the Montblanc de la Culture Award, the first athlete and only unanimous winner in the award's history. But he doesn't do it for the praise.

"I didn't do this to be called a nice guy," he says. "That doesn't mean anything to kids who need help. I want to give this side of town the opportunity to have a top-notch school, and top-notch education is expensive. I learnt that when I was looking for a school for my own son. Something like this is just the beginning."

A further recognition of Robinson's character came in May 2001 when he was presented the NBA Sportsmanship Award, which honours the player who best represents the ideals of sportsmanship on the court. Not surprisingly, Robinson asked the US$25,000 prize to be donated to his school. "It is an honour to join a very distinguised group of individuals," he said. "Along with winning another NBA Championship, seeing the Carver Academy open its doors is one of the great challenges in my life. This donation is going to help move us one step closer to making that happen."

When Robinson joined the NBA, he thought with success would come satisfaction in life - but it didn't. "It was an incredible experience growing in basketball because all of a sudden I became a well-known athlete. All the attention and the hype is deceiving. You think it's going to be great - everybody knows who you are and you get all this attention - but it turns out it is not so incredible. It doesn't give you peace inside. The hype is a fleeting thing; the money and all those things are so short-lived. It's not satisfying because you've got to wake up, look at yourself in the mirror and say, 'Who am I? Where am I going? What am I doing?' And a lot of times you don't have answers for those questions."

These questions weighed heavily upon David. "I felt an emptiness and said to myself, 'There's got to be more to it than this.' I figured maybe it's spiritual. My mother was a Christian and I always figured I was a Christian because she was, like it's a kind of hereditary thing. I told myself, 'Yeah, I'm a Christian.'"

Flying home from the 1986 World Championships in Spain, Robinson was approached by an evangelist who discussed the gospel with him. "I prayed, but didn't understand what he was trying to tell me, so my life didn't change. I just figured, 'Well now I'm really a Christian.'"

When David got to the NBA he still thought he was a Christian, after all he was a pretty good guy. But in 1991, there was a turning point in his relationship with Christ when a minister spoke to him.

"He showed me I didn't have a heart toward God. He convicted me that day. God had given me everything I could think of, yet I never had given him any appreciation for it. That day I just said, 'This is it - everything I give back to you.' He has blessed me a hundred times. He began to open my eyes and teach me.

"Your eyes get opened and you say, 'Wow, all these things happened and led me right to this place. Now I understand why some of these things happened, I understand why I am the person I am.' It was an incredible position to be in. The day before all I was concerned about were my contracts, my houses, my cars, my money and my glorification, the next day I was looking at the Lord and saying, 'How do you want me to use this? What do you want me to do? Where do I need to go?' Everything began to fall into place.

"The world thinks you're nothing if you don't win a championship or if you don't get an MVP award, but for me that's a joke. I look at these guys I face everyday in the locker room - everyday on the court - and I want to see them know what I know. I want to see these guys enjoy life the way I'm able to enjoy life.

"One of my favourite verses in the Bible, John 3:16 says, 'For God so loved the world that he gave his only son, so that whoever believes in him shall not perish but have eternal life.' That is the centre-piece of the Bible - that is exactly what it's all about.

"We've got to understand who God is. He has created everything, including us as his children. He wants nothing but the best for us. As a father, he loves us beyond anything we can imagine. He says, 'I love you. I gave my Son for you, so that you can come back and be my child again. You can't know me unless you know my Son, Jesus Christ. You can't know me unless you know what I've done for you, because it's the greatest act of love ever.'

"When we begin to understand what God did for us, that he gave his Son for us, then our heart is broken everyday. Everyday I wake up, I think about how he was pierced, how he hung on that cross, and I just say: 'Lord, what an awesome gift. What an awesome, awesome gift. And if you love me that much, then I know you must have great things in store for me.'

"When you realise that and your heart is broken, then you need to talk to him and say: 'Lord, I have sinned, but from here on out I want to honour you as my father; I want to honour you as the giver of everything in my life. Please let me start all over. Give me a new life through Jesus Christ. I recognise what you did, I recognise that you gave your Son for me, and everyday of my life I'll try to honour you for that gift.'"

David Robinson's words testify to what his drive in basketball is - not to bring glory to himself but God. "I feel I have an unbelievable responsibility to honour what God has given me. It's far more than what I feel toward the fans and it's far more than what I feel toward the people that pay me, or even my teammates. I have a responsibility to come out and work and make myself better and better, not for my glory and honour but his."

When David Robinson set out from the streets of Virginia, he didn't know what he was looking for. But amongst 20,000 points and 10,000 rebounds in 1,000 NBA games, he found it. And it is this reality he seeks to express in all his actions.

JASON ROBINSON

I HAVE A DREAM

When a friend told Jason Robinson he had a dream about him, he was amused and asked what the dream was about. "I could see you standing on top of the world. You had the world at your feet but gradually the world started crumbling beneath your feet." Jason was amazed. It was uncannily true.

Robinson was on top of the world. He was twenty-one. He had fame and fortune as an international rugby league player - but inside was empty. On the outside things looked great, but inside his life was in a mess. He got by with the help of a bottle.

The dream stopped him in his tracks.

Jason grew up in Leeds and started playing rugby league at school when he was ten. Quite soon he realized he had talent, and by fifteen began wondering if he might one day be good enough to play professionally. Two years later he stopped wondering when the Wigan Rugby League Club offered him a contract.

Jason's childhood included the occasional visit to Sunday School – "just because you got a free lollypop for going." On another occasion he recalls being in church and having nothing to put in the offering. To cover his embarrassment he put one hand over the plate and gave it a little shake with the other to make it sound like a coin being dropped. God was irrelevant to Jason's life.

Wigan was not just any professional rugby league club - it was *the* rugby league club. When Jason signed in 1991, it had won the championship the last two years and the Challenge Cup for the last three.

Jason spent the 1991-92 season learning his trade. He played for the Academy (under-eighteen) and a handful of games in the A team. There was a seven-a-side tournament at the start of the next season and coach John Monie included Jason. He liked what he saw and Jason was picked for the first team at the start of the 1992-93 season – a spot he never lost in his eight years at the club.

Wigan's success continued. There were championship wins in 1993, 1994, 1995 and 1996. There were Challenge Cup wins in 1993, 1994 and 1995 - to say nothing of Premiership, John Player Trophy and Charity Shield wins.

Jason has nothing but praise for the Wigan set-up. "The money in the club was key in enabling it to attract the best players and permitting them to be full-time when a lot of other clubs were part-time. The players who were bought were very motivated. There was always competition for places and that brought out the best in everyone, not only in matches but also in training."

In his first season in the top team, Jason scored thirteen tries, played in the Challenge Cup final at Wembley and made his debut for Great Britain scoring two tries against New Zealand.

The match that gave Jason most satisfaction was the World Club Challenge against Brisbane in Australia in 1994. "It wasn't the best Wigan team I have played in. We were written off by the experts who were even predicting the margin of Brisbane's victory. It was a massive match before a full house of 60,000 and we produced the goods on the day. It was an amazing experience beating them on their own turf."

In 1994 the Wigan players heard the club had signed New Zealand All Black star, Va'aiga Tuigamala. Jason recalls, "We knew he was a good player but beyond that we didn't know much about him. We heard he was a born-again Christian and were interested to see how that would work out."

Jason didn't realise the impact Inga would have on his life over the next few years. "I observed him for a few months. He was different from the rest of us. We would be out drinking a lot; our talk was different and our way of life. What struck me most was that he was such a happy guy. He was at peace with himself. He had something special about him. I didn't quite know what it was, but I knew he had something I wanted.

"He never pushed his views on me, but if I ever wanted someone to talk to he would be there for me. He spoke by how he lived much more than by anything he said."

It was Inga who had the dream about Jason.

"I was extremely successful at my job," Robinson says. "I was financially secure. I had everything material I could want, but I had relationship problems. I did have the world at my feet but surely and certainly it was crumbling. I was having great success on the park but off it my problems were overpowering me.

"It got to the stage where I would be out drinking six nights a week. On the outside everything was great. I was earning a lot of money. I had a fast car, nice clothes. People wanted to associate with me. People wanted what I had, but inside I was empty. I was searching for something. I was looking for happiness in money, in possessions, in drinking, in relationships. But none of these could fill the space within me.

"Drinking was a vicious circle. I had problems so I drank, yet the more I drank, the more problems I had, and the more problems I had, the more I drank. I was getting away with it because on the field I was playing as well as ever.

"I started a relationship with a girl called Amanda. We split up because of my drinking, but she was pregnant. This brought things to a head."

Some time after they had split up, Amanda phoned Jason and got stuck into him, telling him what she thought of him and how he had messed her up. Jason was not particularly sympathetic. About a week later Amanda rang again.

"She got stuck into me again and told me things that were true but that I didn't want to hear or accept. But this time I was convicted by what she said. For the first time I saw clearly the mess I had caused and the hurt I had caused to other people. I could see myself for exactly what I was. It was a painful experience."

That night Jason hardly slept. Throughout the night he wept and wept. Part of it was self-pity but part of it was a genuine desire to change. For the first time he realised he could not go on living as he was.

"I knew it wasn't right. I knew there must be more to life than working all week and drinking every night. The pleasures were very short-lived. It was just a quick fix.

"Next morning I was still in a state. I rang a friend who was a Christian and said, 'I can't go on like this. I don't want to live like this. I need help.' He invited me around to his office and I went immediately. He asked, 'Do you want to invite Jesus into your heart?'

"I knew I could not continue what I was doing. That morning I asked Jesus into my life. The words from the Bible: 'Come to me, all you who are weary and burdened, and I will give you rest' (Matthew 11:28), summed up exactly how I was feeling. At that moment, when I gave my life to the Lord, I felt a burden lifted. I went out of the office that morning smiling. That was the last thing I had thought I would be doing for a while."

Amanda was a Christian but had let her faith drift. When she and Jason split up she went back to church. She needed some support in her problems and found it in the church fellowship. Jason's conversion to Christ happened about two weeks before the baby was due. He wrote to Amanda and told her what had happened, and offered her help.

Amanda initially doubted whether Jason would change but agreed to meet him. Not surprisingly Amanda, having been hurt once, was not about to put herself in a position to be hurt again. Over time things got better.

"It was a miracle. We got back together a week before the child was born, and seven months later we got married. The Lord turned something which was looking so negative into something positive."

Jason made a new start but the problems were still there. He had a court appearance hanging over him at the time. He knew he had things that needed dealing with. For a start, there was drinking. At first he tried going out with friends and not drinking, but inevitably he would get sucked into his old ways. Eventually he decided he had to cut himself off from some of his old friends.

A book he read challenged him. "It said you couldn't sit on the fence. You either go God's way or the devil's. It was a big kick up the backside for me. I knew my way was leading nowhere. I thought it through and decided on God's way.

"It wasn't easy. It took about two months. It is the hardest thing I've ever done. It was a sacrifice, but also the best thing I've done. It has given me a purpose, knowing that I have something to live for and something to aim for in life. There is the security and peace of knowing that when all this is done, I know where I'm going. I don't believe when you come to Christ all your problems disappear overnight. We still have problems but the Lord helps us get through them."

Jason dealt with the drinking problem. From that day, in 1995, he has never been in a pub to drink socially. He still drinks at home, a glass of wine with a meal, but pubs are a thing of the past.

Deciding to follow Christ in your life is one thing; representing Christ to all your friends is quite a different challenge. "For four years I had been one of the lads, bragging how much beer I could drink, how many girls I had had, the kind of car I drove and so on. Suddenly I turned around and said 'I am a Christian'. I'm sure they were thinking, 'Yeah, we will give you a week.' I was determined to prove them wrong. The Lord didn't take me away from rugby and the people I used to go out with. He has kept me in the same situation but has strengthened me and made me a witness for him.

"It hasn't been easy but I am proud to say I believe in Christ. The best way to be a witness is by how you live, and I hope I show people, by the things I do and say or the things I don't say, who I follow and the things I stand for."

One particular outworking of Jason's conversion to Christianity was a concern for the homeless. He and some friends helped the homeless in Manchester. "Some friends from the church and I had it on our hearts to help them. We started off just making some sandwiches and taking some flasks out to the streets of

Manchester. We gave homeless people some sandwiches and tried to be there for them, to show them that someone cared about them and tried to tell them about Jesus as well.

"Things developed. Someone lent us a van and we got food from Tesco. As we got bigger we were able to help more and raised some money, had a mobile catering unit like a burger van and made tea and coffee, which made it easier for us. It is probably the most rewarding thing I have done."

Playing for Wigan as a Christian, Jason's career continued to prosper. He played a dozen times for Great Britain plus seven times for England scoring thirteen international tries, including a record of scoring a try in six consecutive Great Britain games.

In 1995 Wigan beat Leeds in the Challenge Cup final with Jason collecting the Lance Todd trophy as Man-of-the-Match after scoring two tries in the 30-10 win.

That same year, Jason played for Great Britain in the Rugby League World Cup. In the first match Britain met Australia. With the score 10-all, Jason pounced on a loose ball to score. Great Britain went on to win, 20-16. Next, Britain beat Fiji, 46-0, with Jason scoring two tries. He did not play in the win over South Africa, but was back for the semi-final when Wales were defeated, 25-10. In the final, Australia turned the tables with a 16-8 victory, but there were only two points in it with fifteen minutes to go.

"We beat Australia in the group stage, but as two teams went through the Aussies qualified with us. We reached the final and met Australia again and unfortunately they won. It was a good experience to play in the World Cup and overall I thought we did well coming so close to winning it."

In the autumn of 1996 Jason was under contract to the Australian Rugby League and found himself free in the off-season, when he was approached to play rugby union for Bath. The only problem was that he had never played rugby and was quite unfamiliar with the game. "It was a good experience but I did not know the rules at all. I was thrown in at the deep end, playing two matches a week. I got quite a bit of criticism but, given that I did not know the rules and had never played it before, I thought I did pretty well."

In 1998, the Challenge Cup final between Wigan and Sheffield didn't go according to the script. "Everyone expected us to win. People were saying beforehand we could give Sheffield a thirty-point start and still beat them. Shortly after the final we beat them 36-6 in the League, but on the day Sheffield produced a display they would probably never be able to do again. It was great for Sheffield, and great for rugby league, but it was probably my worst moment in rugby league."

By the end of 2000, Jason had played four winter and five summer seasons for Wigan, a total of 283 appearances in which he had scored 173 tries. An offer came to switch codes and play rugby union for Sale Sharks in Manchester. It wasn't an easy decision. He was at the peak of his career as a rugby league player.

"A major reason for coming to Sale," he explains, "was that I believe God has pointed me this way. It didn't just happen overnight; I prayed for the Lord's guidance over six months. I had done everything in rugby league that it was possible to do, but now the Lord had given me a new challenge."

After just ten games for Sale, with four tries, Jason was called up to the England squad. On February 17, 2001 he made his debut during England's record breaking 80-23 point victory over Italy in the Six Nations at Twickenham, becoming the first English player to switch from league to union and earn international caps in both codes.

"It was a great feeling running out in front of a 75,000 full house at Twickenham," Robinson said after the game. "I was really encouraged to hear that roar. I didn't know how the public would take to me because the switch was still only recent, but it was a great moment and a fantastic atmosphere."

A further honour came after just three international appearances for England, when Robinson was named to the British and Irish Lions squad for a tour of Australia in mid-2001. The wing's Lions debut couldn't have been more impressive, crossing the line five times during a tour match against the Queensland Presidents XV. "It is always good to score tries when you are a winger," Robinson said. "I've only scored five once before, and that was for Wigan against Leeds." Coach Graham Henry joked, "He likes scoring tries doesn't he?"

The selectors were so impressed by Robinson's haul they rewarded him with a start in the first test against Australia. Again the rugby convert repaid their faith, claiming the opening try in the second minute. The World Champion Wallabies were overwhelmed by the Lions' display, the final score an upset 29-13.

Robinson returned from the tour recognised as one of the most potent attacking players in international rugby, having proven his abilities were not limited to just league. "Reflecting on the tour," he said, "I was very happy with my own personal contribution. To score five tries on my Lions debut was brilliant – you could not have dreamt that things would have gone as they did. It was also great that I played in every Test match – scoring the first try in the opening and last Test. Overall coming to Australia and scoring ten tries has been brilliant along with the invaluable experience that I have picked up."

Robinson's added experience showed when he returned to play for England. In November, the side was in record-breaking form as it smashed Romania 134-0, running in twenty tries to post its highest ever international score, Robinson personally responsible for twenty of the points.

"I was quite relieved to finally touch down for England," he said. "I was hoping I would be able to get my first try, otherwise it would have been six games and no tries. Having got the first one it turned out to be a good day. The final tally brought me up to four in six games."

Jason increased his tally to six tries in eight England appearances with two tries in the opening fourteen minutes against Scotland. *The Daily Telegraph* in London wrote after the 29-3 victory: "In darker days Jason Robinson found God. But was after God had found Jason Robinson, and endowed him with the talent that cut Scotland to bits at the weekend.

"Robinson is the small man's Jonah Lomu. The effect on the crowd of him gathering a pass in open country is similarly profound. Awe, dread and exhilaration surge through spectators, even the ones on the receiving end. The Scots need feel no shame about having that guilty secret. It is an obligatory response to destructive genius. For the home crowd on Saturday, watching their team impaled by Robinson's two unstoppable first-half runs, the pleasure of seeing talent do its thing might just have softened the pain of defeat. They lost the match, but gained some boasting rights. They saw rugby's essence on the hoof...

"As even this famously partisan Murrayfield crowd understood, what Robinson embodies is the irrepressibility of talent. League, union: he renders the distinction worthless."

Despite his short time in rugby, Robinson has already become part of the game's elite and is certain to be part of the English and Lions sides for several years. But there is another team to which Robinson belongs, and he is certain to be part of it for eternity. His membership is this team comes not through his abilities or anything he has done, but through his faith in Jesus Christ's death on the cross in his place. "For God so loved the world that he gave his one and only Son, that whoever believes in him shall not perish but have eternal life." (John 3:36).

This chapter was written with Stuart Weir

CLAUDIO TAFFAREL

SAINT TAFFAREL

The sun broke through the clouds on a muggy day in mid-July 1994, shining on the Rose Bowl in Pasadena, just over ten kilometres from downtown Los Angeles. Inside the stadium, over 94,000 people were silenced by nervous anticipation. Around the globe, billions watched their televisions as the world's biggest sporting event approached its conclusion. In the middle of it all were Brazilian goalkeeper Claudio Taffarel and Italian striker Roberto Baggio.

Everyone anticipated that Brazil would win the 1994 soccer World Cup but, after ninety minutes of normal time, the game was a scoreless tie. The sides continued on the field for another thirty minutes, but again time finished with the scoreboard unchanged at nil-all. The final was to be decided by penalty kicks. Throughout the tournament, followers of the game were sure the boot of Brazilian striker, Romario, would seal the victory, but now all hopes rested upon the team's goalie, Claudio Taffarel.

Like most boys from his country, Taffarel always played soccer, but either basketball or volleyball was where he hoped to make his mark. He tried hard, but as he realised he couldn't match the skill of other players, his determination began to wane. In 1984, Claudio decided to give soccer a shot.

"I liked sport, but didn't know in what position I could best express myself. One day I went to Porto Alegre International and went straight to the goals and asked to be tried out," he says. One year later, he turned professional.

Over the years with both club and national sides, he had success: World Junior Champion in 1985; Silver medallist at the Seoul Olympics in 1988; Italian Champion in 1992; European Champion (UEFA Cup) in 1993 and 2000; World Champion in 1994; and Copa America Champion in 1997. Claudio has also worn the number one jersey for Brazil in three World Cups.

Despite it being his favourite position, the Brazilian thinks being a goalie is one of the hardest positions on the field. "If you have a good defensive line," he explains, "that makes your job easier, but the pressure is still there. You have to assume your defense will be penetrated and it's at those moments when your actions alone may determine the difference between a win and loss. Also, many times it is the goalkeeper who is blamed when a team loses. However, it is a rare occasion when the goalkeeper is credited with the team's victory. People only see the middle of the field, no one pays attention to the goalkeeper."

The Brazilian press didn't wanting Taffarel as their team's goalkeeper during the 1994 World Cup, but he woke up relaxed on the morning of the final. "'I felt calm and confident," he says. "I felt as if I was going to play a pre-season game and not the final of the World Cup against Italy. Something different was happening inside of me. We went to the stadium with enormous confidence. As we entered the tunnel that led to the field, I noticed the Italian players were insecure and despondent, while our team hollered, 'Let's go, let's win.'

"When the game and the overtime ended in a tie and we went to penalty kicks, I remembered the words I had studied that week: 'We wait in hope for the Lord; he is our help and our shield. In him our hearts rejoice, for we trust in his holy name. May your unfailing love rest upon us, O Lord, even as we put our hope in you.'" (Psalm 33: 20-22)

Taffarel became a Christian just after turning professional. "I was playing with Brazil's Junior League team and began attending the Bible study for athletes. They spoke about God in a very intimate and humble manner.

"I became interested as the prospect of happiness and peace was discussed. After hearing a lot about Jesus, I understood that only he could give me the satisfaction I had dreamt of for so long, that it was he who would guide my life according to his wishes. I accepted his death for me as the only way to salvation. I confessed my sins and began following his teachings.

"The verse in the Bible: 'Draw near to God, and he will draw near to you' (James 4: 8) spoke to me. There was no big change at first, but gradually I looked at myself and I was changing from the inside.

"At first, I felt embarrassed when I was asked if I was a follower of Christ, but the Lord was merciful to me. He allowed the transformation of my life to happen little by little. Today, I'm happy to proclaim the Lord's name.

"Ever since I invited Jesus Christ to live in my heart I began to count on the strength, the love and the power of God in the most important moments of my life. Not everything is a bed of roses in the Christian's life - and for me it was no different. When the going gets tough, when one is double-crossed by coaches and team administrators, when I let an easy ball get by me for a goal, when the fans are booing me, when I lost my dad or when I saw my wife between life and death in the Intensive Care Unit of a hospital in Porto Alegre, when it was time to stop those decisive penalty kicks - I realised how important it is to not be alone. God never left me high and dry, and it wasn't any different in the final of the World Cup in 1994."

Via satellite half of the population of the planet was watching. The tension was rising. "Halfway through the penalty kicks I looked at the scoreboard and saw we were tied, two-all. I knew it was my turn to do something for my country and my team.

"I prayed, 'Lord, now is the time for me to defend against these penalty kicks. Please help me catch this one.' The Lord granted my request. When Massaro kicked, I think God pushed me to the left side and I was able to stop the ball. Then Dunga scored for Brazil and we were down to the final kick.

"Fifty-two games had been played, three million tickets had been sold, four years of preparation and one month of hype in the media around the whole world and the final decision of all this came down to the two of us: Baggio and me. When I saw him with his head down and staring at the ground, I realised he was insecure and my confidence soared. At that moment, I was sure of one thing: either I was going to make the save or he was going to miss his penalty kick."

Baggio placed the ball on the dot, looked at the goal, breathing to himself. He walked back from the ball, considering his shot. Running in, he swung his leg at the ball, contacting it with his foot. The ball spun through the air as it sailed towards the goal. Taffarel followed its trajectory with his body and eyes, joined by billions everywhere, as it travelled over the cross bar. Victory was Brazil's.

"When that ball went flying high over the cross bar, the only thing I wanted to do was kneel and glorify God, because I knew the victory came from him and only he deserved the glory. In the end, neither Baggio made the goal nor I stopped the ball in the final play of the World Cup of 1994.

"In all of this, I learnt it is much better to trust in someone who is infinitely more powerful than us - someone who loves us, who understands us, who helps us and cares about every detail of our lives. His name is Jesus and he's the only way that leads to God. He is the truth in a world filled with lies."

In 1998, at the World Cup in France, it again came down to penalty kicks, but this time in the semi-final. Playing against the Dutch, the scores were equal at one a piece at the end of regular and extra time. Maintaining a reputation that has lead to him being referred to as "Saint Taffarel", the keeper saved two of the oppositions strikes and led Brazil into the final with a four-two win. After the game his nation's president, Fernando Henrique Cardoso, wrote to the team: "Our sincere thanks to Taffarel in the name of every Brazilian."

Unfortunately, the president would not have been in the same joyous mood one week later as the Brazilians went down to France in a shock three-nil result in the final. That was Taffarel's last game for Brazil, his career ending after 101 games. With Taffarel in the goals, the team lost just twelve times and went unbeaten for twenty-three games from August 1993 until April 1997. In his ten years, the goalie let in just seventy goals.

Two years later the UEFA Cup final remained scoreless after 120 minutes. Taffarel stood in the goals for Galatasaray, facing Arsenal's best strikers. The veteran was traded to the Turkish club in 1998 on the back of his reputation a one of the world's finest keepers. Now was the chance to prove his worth.

With anyone else guarding the net, the Galatasaray fans would be justified in being nervous, instead they were content knowing Taffarel had been there before and done it before. He didn't let them down, conceding only one goal as his team posted a four-one victory. The win gave Galatasaray the rare triple of a European title, and domestic league and cup titles. It was also the first time a Turkish club had won a European title.

Taffarel has experienced the highs of winning, but this is not where his strength lies. "My greatest joy as a professional," he says, "was to win the World Cup in the United States in 1994.

But after a few days, the memories began to fade away, as do all things in life. But my relationship with God will never fade away."

Claudio's strength rests upon his relationship with Jesus Christ. He may not play in any more World Cups or produce amazing saves to clinch Brazil a victory, but he knows his future is secure with God.

This chapter was written with the help of Alex Ribeiro

K U R T W A R N E R

FIRST THINGS FIRST

Kurt Warner began the 1999 NFL season unknown, six months later he was the biggest name in the league, becoming the Most Valuable Player of season and the Super Bowl. In his first year as a starter he lifted the St. Louis Rams from the bottom rung of the league ladder to Super Bowl champions.

Warner's journey to NFL success started in Iowa where he was an All-State representative in both football and basketball in his senior year at Regis High School. Kurt received a part-scholarship with the Division I-AA University of Northern Iowa for football, but sat on the bench throughout college until his senior year when he led UNI to the playoffs and was the Gateway Conference offensive player of the year.

After an impressive college season Warner hoped to catch the eye of an NFL team, but was passed over in the draft. Green Bay however decided to sign him as an undrafted free agent for $5,000. After getting just fourteen reps in five weeks training, he was cut.

"I was devastated," Warner says. "When the Packers cut me I suddenly had to confront my future. Giving up on football wasn't an option, so I tried to come up with a plan that would put me in the best position to make it back to the NFL. I had my immediate sights on the World League – now called NFL Europe – which serves as sort of a farm league for NFL teams while fanning pro football's popularity overseas."

Again Warner was passed over. With his dreams of football greatness slipping away, the only job he could get was in an all-night grocery store. "That's just about as humbled as you can get," he says, "to go from being in an NFL camp, where you're treated like a king and have a contract for a couple of hundred thousand dollars if you make the team, to stocking shelves for $5.50 an hour."

In March 1995, after six months working in the store, Warner signed with the Iowa Barnstormers in the Arena League, which by his own admission "looked sort of low budget and strange."

Over the following three seasons, Kurt passed for 10,164 yards and 183 touchdowns with the Barnstormers, leading them to Arena Bowl appearances in his last two years. In 1997, he completed sixty-five percent of his passes for 4,149 yards and 79 touchdowns, becoming the third quarterback in the history of the league to pass for over 4,000 yards.

In September 1997, the Chicago Bears approached Warner to tryout. More than three years after being cut by Green Bay, he was getting another shot at the NFL. First Warner had to take care of his wedding to Brenda Meoni and their honeymoon in October.

On the second last day of the honeymoon, Kurt was bitten by something on the elbow and it swelled up to the size of a baseball. Warner was due to fly to Chicago the day after returning, but when he got home his elbow was still swollen. He called the Bears to postpone the tryout, and even though they said they'd be in touch, Kurt never heard back.

Two months later Warner secured a workout with the St. Louis Rams. "I had the worst workout of my life," he says. "I was awful, just abysmal. The thumb I had broken in my final season of Arena ball hadn't quite healed yet, but I assumed it wouldn't be a problem. Bad assumption: I had trouble gripping the ball, and couldn't hit the broad side of a barn. Accuracy has always been my strong suit, the thing I felt could set me apart, and now I was totally erratic. I figured I was done."

Despite his performance, the Rams recognised Warner's ability and signed him two days before Christmas, deciding to allocate him to the Amsterdam Admirals in NFL Europe for 1998. Playing in Europe meant being away from his family and pregnant wife, but it also gave him another shot at his dream.

Warner had a successful year, winning seven of his nine starts. Despite missing one game he led the league in passing yards (2,101), attempts (326), completions (165) and touchdowns (15).

Kurt returned from Amsterdam and reported to the Rams in June 1998, where he and another quarterback fought for the third-string position. Tony Banks was the team's starter and Steve Bono had been signed as a veteran backup, leaving one shot available.

In late August, well into the night before the final roster-cutdown deadline, the Rams decided to go with Warner. "I was pumped up beyond belief," he says. "Finally I had made it to the bigs, and I had no intention of stopping there."

Warner sat on the bench throughout the season until the final game against the San Francisco 49ers, making his NFL debut with 3:38 remaining. He was on the field for two drives, completing four of eleven passes for thirty-nine yards.

For the 1999 season St. Louis cut Tony Banks and Steve Bono, signed Trent Green as the starting quarterback and elevated Kurt to second-string. In an exhibition game against the San Diego Chargers, Green went down with a season-ending knee injury. The team was devastated, but it provided Warner with an opportunity to become the starting quarterback.

Without Green the Rams were expected to repeat their disappointing performances of 1998, entering the season with the worst record of any NFL team in the nineties. Despite this, Warner led his team to a 27-10 season opening win against the Baltimore Ravens, throwing for 309 yards and three touchdowns.

St. Louis' good start continued with victory over the Atlanta Falcons, Warner again throwing three touchdowns. The Rams made it three in a row when they travelled to Cincinnati. Warner's passer rating for the game was a perfect 158.3, aided by three touchdowns and 310 yards, the quarterback becoming the first person in fifty years to throw three touchdowns in each of his first three starts.

The first big test of the season came in the fourth week against the San Francisco 49ers, as attention began to focus on St. Louis and its quarterback. In the first quarter, Warner had thrown for 177 yards and three touchdowns.

"It seemed like everything was happening in slow motion," Kurt says. "My line gave me a ton of time, my passes were perfect, and my receivers were wide open. I don't think the 49ers knew what hit them; they had no idea what we were capable of until that point."

The Rams won 42-20, Warner completing twenty of twenty-three passes for 323 yards and five touchdowns; his touchdown tally already fourteen from just four games – more than all the team's quarterbacks had thrown the previous season.

"Our next game was a rematch with the Falcons in Atlanta, and that was probably my toughest week of the season. Now it seemed like everyone wanted a piece of me. I could understand how it was a big story, but at that point it had been told and retold several times and even I was getting bored by it. When you're growing up you always think how cool it would be to see yourself on TV; now I was so sick of myself I'd reach for the remote. It was hard to stay as focused as I needed to be, and I had a lousy week of practice."

Despite the distractions, the Rams picked up their fifth win. The Cleveland Browns became victim number six the following week, Warner back in form with another three-touchdown haul.

St. Louis couldn't make it seven in a row, even with 328 yards to Warner. The team fought back from 21-0 down against the Tennessee Titans but fell three points short, losing 21-24.

"We were devastated," Warner says. "You'd have thought we'd lost a playoff game. That was yet another sign our attitude had undergone a makeover. We were convinced we were the better team and bemoaned our missed opportunity. But as a day or two removed from the disappointment, we began to appreciate the mettle we had displayed."

The Rams' woes continued the following week against the Detroit Lions, conceding a touchdown in the final minute to go down 27-31. "The guys were like zombies after the game, not only in the locker room but for the next couple of days too.

"Now the skeptics were out in full force. Halfway through the season, we had played just two teams with winning records and lost to both of them. But we were hardly demoralized. We felt we should have won both of those games, and we still believed we were a very good team."

Over the following seven weeks the Rams showed how good they were, winning all their games. The streak started with a twenty-five point thrashing of the Carolina Panthers, the list of defeated teams growing every week: San Francisco (23-7), the New Orleans Saints (43-12), the Panthers again (34-21), the Saints again (30-14), the New York Giants (31-10) and Chicago (34-12).

Unfortunately, St. Louis couldn't close out the season against the Philadelphia Eagles. Despite the loss, the Rams finished with a season record of thirteen wins, three loses; and secured home births for the playoffs. Warner was also named the NFL's Most Valuable Player, and threw forty-one touchdowns to join Dan Marino as the only quarterback to tally more than forty in one season.

Rested after a first round bye, the Rams played the Minnesota Vikings in their first playoff game. Warner guided his side to a 49-17 lead before the Vikings clawed back twenty points in the last five minutes. Despite the late charge, it was a comfortable win, Kurt finishing with 391 yards and five touchdowns.

Next it was the NFC Championship game against the Tampa Bay Buccaneers, one last hurdle before the Super Bowl. St. Louis ground out an 11-6 win, sealed with a touchdown in the final five minutes.

"Now the ultimate game was in our direct line of vision," the quarterback says. "It was just amazing to realise where we had come from and how far we had travelled to get to that point. It was too much to fathom."

The following day the Rams were on a plane to Atlanta for Super Bowl XXXIV, preparing to battle the Titans who had beaten them earlier in the season. Game day came, and Warner helped his team to a 16-0 lead, but Tennessee fought back to level at 16-all with two minutes and twelve seconds remaining.

"I began to pray – for focus, for strength, for protection. I'm a man who is driven by faith, and any power or peace I feel, on the football field or otherwise, is because of my faith and my relationship with Jesus."

Warner recognises a lot of people are turned off when athletes talk like this. "I'm not trying to preach," he says, "or be overly judgmental, and I'm not in any way claiming that God is some sort of football grand pooh-bah who hands out touchdowns and sacks to the faithful like winning lottery tickets. I'm just trying to give people a sense of what works for me and how it has helped me achieve success in sports and in much more important endeavours. To put it simply, any sharpness, clarity, and grace under fire I'm able to summon are a result of faith and God's presence in my life."

The quarterback needed all the strength he could muster. Not only was he exhausted, having already passed forty-four times including a record thirty-five in the first half, but he was also suffering a rib injury from just before the main break.

"999 H-Balloon" was called, and the Rams set for the play that could seal them victory. The ball fired back to Warner. Looking down the field he saw Isaac Bruce and let the ball rip before Jevon "The Freak" Kearse sent him to the deck.

"After I fell, I looked up in time to see Ike come back and catch the underthrown pass just in front of the off-balance Denard Walker. Then there were bodies in front of me, but I could tell from the way the fans were screaming that something good had happened. Ike made a beautiful move, and that was it. I got to my feet just as he was charging into the end zone, and I started sprinting down there to join the celebration."

The conversion went through and the Rams were up 23-16. Warner had done his job and now it was up to the defence to keep Tennessee out. At the time he was unaware he had just broken Joe Montana's Super Bowl record with 414 passing yards.

"I stood alone on the sidelines, my heart racing. When I was in control, when I knew I'd have the ball in my hands, I felt so peaceful and secure. But now there was nothing I could do but watch as our extremely exhausted defensive players tried to hang on."

The Titan's worked down the field. Steve McNair found Kevin Dyson who charged towards the end zone. "From where I was," Warner remembers, "the space in front of him seemed wide open, and it looked like he was going to walk in easily for a touchdown. Out of nowhere I saw Mike Jones, our middle linebacker, burst into the frame. Then, with no one else in the vicinity, Mike made a tackle that every high school football coach in America should show to his players.

"I've seen the replay a few dozen times by now, and the more I watch it, the more I appreciate the beauty of Mike's stop. Nine times out of ten, Dyson's momentum would have carried him into the end zone, but Mike just made an unbelievable tackle. Right place, right time, right technique: he grabbed one foot and then kicked the other knee out from underneath, so Dyson had no feet left. If Mike had missed that second foot, I think Dyson would've taken another step and reached that extra yard to cross the plane of the goal line, but Mike managed to take him straight down."

The Rams had won. "I looked at the clock and made sure time had expired," Warner adds. "The inside of my body exploded with rapture, and I rushed onto the field to join the party."

Kurt was escorted to the victory dais to receive the Lombardi Trophy and do interviews. The ABC's Mike Tirico said, "First things first – tell me about the final touchdown pass to Isaac." The quarterback answered, "Well, first things first, I've got to thank my Lord and Saviour up above – thank you, Jesus."

"I'm well aware that an athlete who thanks Jesus after a victory turns some people off," Warner explains, "but I'm not thanking him so much because I threw a lot of touchdowns or my team won the game, but because of the incredible effect he has had on my life. If anyone would ask, I'd gladly thank him after every bitter defeat too, because the feelings I'm expressing are far bigger than football."

Kurt became a Christian through the help of his wife, Brenda. Before they were married, she often challenged him about his faith. "I took real offence to that," Warner says, "because I still believed what I'd always believed: that being a Christian meant being a good person and doing your best to follow the Ten Commandments and always trying to do the right thing."

Warner was also being challenged by Christians in his team, and over time thought about what they were saying. "I didn't have the sense of hope and peace and assurance Brenda and my Christian friends had in their faith.

"There was no single, magic moment where I shed my skin and emerged anew. Instead, it was a gradual feeling that probably evolved over the course of about ten months. I finally reached the point where I knew what I needed to do."

It wasn't until early 1996, when Brenda's parents were killed by a freak tornado, that Kurt realised he had changed. "You would think that would have been the lowest point imaginable," he says, "yet I actually got closer to God and to Brenda than I ever had been before. I had this new sense of peace within me through the whole experience that actually enabled me to give her spiritual strength and guidance."

Warner continued to grow in his faith, and two years later was leading a team bible study while playing for the Amsterdam Admirals. "I believe the Lord used that experience to stretch and prepare me to become the witness he wanted me to be in the future. God placed me in an unfamiliar and uncomfortable atmosphere, and I had to find a way to get it done through him. It was all part of my evolution as a Christian, and the fact that I was out of my circle of comfort accelerated the process."

Kurt's faith continued to mature as he joined the Rams, and guided him through the whirlwind of the 1999 season. Warner now sees himself was an ambassador for God. "I realise why I'm here," he says. "My role is not just to be successful on the football field but to touch lives and to share my testimony. My hope is to make a difference for Jesus in everything I do."

After winning the Super Bowl, Warner was an obvious selection for the Pro Bowl and led the NFC to victory over the AFC. But the quarterback's miracle season didn't receive its fitting conclusion until July the following year when he signed a seven-year US$46.5 million contract with the Rams, a welcome increase on the $250,000 salary he received for 1999 and a long way from the $5.50 an hour he earned stocking shelves.

With the security of a long-term deal, Kurt kept showing his talent in 2000 even though his season was affected by injury. St. Louis started the season with a run of six wins, Warner unstoppable with seventeen touchdowns and 2260 yards – eclipsing the yardage record for that many games. Against San Diego, he became the only player to ever earn a perfect quarterback rating of 158.3 twice – the feat achieved with twenty-four of thirty passes completed for 390 yards and four touchdowns.

The Rams' winning run was ended by the Kansas City Chiefs, Warner's record-tying streak of six consecutive 300-yard passing games also finished by a broken finger. While its quarterback was sidelined for five weeks, St. Louis suffered three loses. Upon return, Kurt had his worst ever game, throwing a personal record four interceptions to finish with a passer rating on 26.0. "I'll take credit for this loss," he said after the game. "I'm the one out there playing, and when I throw the ball to somebody else that's my fault and no one else's."

With three weeks remaining, Warner returned to near peak form as the Rams beat Minnesota and New Orleans but lost to Tampa Bay by three. After suffering concussion in the final game, Kurt recovered for a postseason rematch with the Saints. Despite three touchdowns and 365 yards from the quarterback, St. Louis went down 28-31, its hopes of a Super Bowl repeat gone.

It would be little more than twelve months until Warner would again find himself in the Super Bowl spotlight though. For the second time in three years the quarterback led his team to the season ending game, again named the NFL's Most Valuable Player – joining only five other players to receive the award twice.

"Let me thank God for the continued blessings in my life," Kurt said after the announcement. "It's amazing what He has done with an ordinary man in such a short period of time. He has blessed me with a very unique and special situation, surrounded by unique and special athletes."

Warner earned the recognition for a remarkable season in which the Rams lost only two of their sixteen games for the best record in the league. He threw for the second-highest single-season passing yard total in NFL history, completing 375 of 546 passes for 4,830 yards and thirty-six touchdowns. Warner also helped his club become the only team in league history to score more than 500 points in three consecutive seasons.

With such an imposing record, St. Louis was a hot favourite for Super Bowl honours and qualified for the game with wins over Green Bay and Philadelphia in the playoffs. Opposing the Rams were the underdog New England Patriots.

Against all predictions, the Patriots built a 17-3 lead – Warner responsible for the opening touchdown when his pass was intercepted and run half the field for the score. St. Louis fought back in the final period to level the game at 17-all, the quarterback first rushing over for a touchdown before passing to Ricky Proehl for another. But with only seconds left on the clock, the Patriots kicked a forty-eight yard field goal for the victory.

In 2000 the fairytale belonged to the Rams, but in 2002 it was New England's turn. "The offense basically gave up the first seventeen points on turnovers," Warner said after the game. "Our defense played well enough to be world champions. And that's what hurts the most – that I let some guys down."

Despite such lows, Kurt's unlikely rise among the NFL's greatest quarterbacks won't be quickly forgotten. But he hopes his most enduring legacy will be for the kingdom of God. "I'm here to do the Lord's work," he says. "I'm not here to make a lot of money or to get fame, I'm here to make a difference for him."

After his naming as the MVP for the second time, Warner summarised: "I have enjoyed the opportunities that the Lord has given me to reach and effect so many lives. I have realised that because of what I do, people want to be more like me. So, I try to spend every day of my life becoming more like Jesus. I have always prayed that the Lord would place me in a position to reach many people for Him and I have tried to seize every opportunity. The greatest benefit of all I have been given is that I can share the love of Jesus and His influence in my life with so many people."

Peter Furst is a Sydney based television sports reporter working for Network Ten. He is the author of three books, and a media graduate of Macquarie University. His chief sporting interests are rugby and cricket.